Song of Eliria

Song of Eliria

Heather Starsong

Dancing Aspen Press

This is a work of fiction. Names, characters, and events described herein are imaginary. Any resemblance to actual events, organizations, or persons, living or dead, is entirely coincidental. The town of Cottonwood Creek and the Compassionate Care Nursing Home are fictitious.

Author: Heather Starsong
Title: *Song of Eliria*
Description: First edition | Boulder, CO: Dancing Aspen Press
Subjects: Fiction, Healing, Family Relationships, Mystery, Romance, Alien contact, Women's literature
Identifiers: ISBN Trade Paperback #978-0-9975450-2-9
         ISBN eBook #978-0-9975450-3-6
Library of Congress Control Number: 2019914348

Table of Contents

Chapter 1

ℳoonrise

The jagged peaks of the foothills jutted black against an indigo sky pierced with the diamond brilliance of winter stars. Tucked between the foothills and the city of Boulder, a trail looped around a frozen lake. A lone figure limped along it.

Even as she leaned heavily on her walking stick, Harriet held her tall, spare body upright. Cold stung her nostrils. Step by step she went forward. Each step was a jab of pain—sharp, bitter, shooting up into her hip. Her lower lip was caught between her teeth, all her being focused on taking the next step.

She hadn't thought to bring a flashlight, but the whiteness of the snow and the glow of the city reflected in the sky gave her enough light to find her way. Even in the dim light, the trail was clear, the snow trampled by all the people who walked there during the day. She, too, had walked there almost daily, in spite of the pain, seeking the peace of hills, trees, sky, and water.

There was no peace now, only the raging grief in her heart and the stabbing agony in her leg. Over the last two years, all that had meaning for her, all the joy and purpose in her life, had slipped away through the sieve of pain, leaving behind only the dark lumps of loneliness, fear, and desperation.

On the west side of the lake, a narrow path left the main trail and climbed the ridge. She had just turned onto that path when she heard men's voices behind her. Panic jolted her. She spun around, looking for a place to hide. A few steps up the ridge path, a small wooden bridge crossed an irrigation ditch. She ran to it, dropped to her knees, and, stifling a cry of pain, half rolled, half fell into the ditch and scrambled under the bridge.

In summer it was lovely to sit by the ditch and watch the movement of the water, the leaf shadows dancing across it. Now it was full of snow. She huddled there, barely breathing, praying the men had not seen her, praying they wouldn't notice her footprints verging off the main trail.

The men came closer. She could hear their low, male voices and their footsteps squeaking in the snow. She scrunched deeper into the shadow of the bridge.

One man said, "I sure don't see anyone."

"Who knows what that caller saw," the other man said. "'Limping,' she said. 'Someone in trouble.' If he was limping, we should have caught up with him by now."

The first man gave a brief laugh. "Well, she got us out for a walk on a starry night."

They went by, following the main trail around the lake.

Park rangers. Harriet hadn't known they patrolled at night. Someone in one of the houses near the trail must have seen her and called in. Someone else awake in the wee hours of the morning.

She lay still, curled in a tight ball. Cold seeped into her. She was exhausted, tempted to give up and just hide there.

No. It wasn't safe. Someone might find her before … She crawled out of the ditch and pulled herself up with her stick.

The ridge path was harder to see. No one had walked there since the snow the night before. But it was slightly indented, and her feet knew it. She had climbed that path innumerable times before her injury. High up, there was a place she knew, a little way off the path, where the steep rise of the ridge folded into a small hollow shielded by low shrubs. It would be a long time before anyone found her there. Long enough.

She climbed. A few steps. Rested. Caught her breath. Climbed again, leaning heavily on her stick. She slipped and stumbled, gathered herself and pressed on.

Not so long ago she could stride up this trail, stopping only once in a while, not because she was tired, but only to enjoy the view. Now it seemed impossibly steep and endless.

"Keep going," she muttered fiercely to herself. "You can. You can make it."

She stumbled again and fell to her knees. Her stick slipped out of her hand and slid down the hill. She couldn't go on without it. She crouched there, panting, ready to give up. But her navy blue jacket would be too obvious against the snow. Heart pounding, she searched for her stick. It was far below, a dark line against the white hillside. Clinging to some rocks that stuck up out of the snow, she crawled down to retrieve it, lurched to her feet, and continued to climb.

At last. There was the place, just a little farther up and to the left. The lip of the hollow curved out from the hillside, outlined by the shrubs that hid it, the intricate pattern of their bare branches black against the snow.

She left the path, struggled up to the brink of the hollow, and looked into it. The snow lay deep and untouched a few steps below her. Only a few steps and she could lie down and let go. It was so cold she would soon sleep. It would be over.

She turned. One last look at the sky. The cold, brilliant beauty of the stars pierced her.

Will there be stars? she wondered. A tremor ran through her. I don't know. It's all unknown. Will I be punished for taking my life? Is there hell after all? No. I can't believe that.

But maybe there won't be stars.

She lowered her eyes and looked out over the lake below, the city, the plains spreading out beyond, all dimly lit by starlight, snow light, and the glow of the city. Far away the eastern horizon brightened.

The tip of the waning moon appeared above the plains. Time stopped as she watched it rise. Slowly, slowly it cleared the horizon and hung low in the eastern sky, a pale silver sickle. Its light brightened the whiteness of the snow, glistened on the ice on the lake. The night was hushed. The wind still. All was bathed in the magic of moonlight.

She drew in a ragged breath. On the brink of the hollow, on the brink of life and death, she stood clutching her stick, all pain and grief forgotten, drowned in beauty.

She lifted her eyes again to the stars. A shudder ran through her, shaking her whole body. From the depths of her chest, a sob welled up. "I can't," she whispered. She looked back into the hollow behind her, then in a rush, stumbled away from it, down the path, almost running.

Her foot caught and she fell, slipped, then tumbled rolling and sliding, clutching vainly at the slippery slope, a long way, until she came up hard against a boulder protruding from the hillside.

The impact knocked the breath out of her and she lay stunned, sprawled in the snow.

No. No, she prayed. I don't want to die yet. I can go on. I *have* gone on, day by day in spite of the pain. I have seen my patients, taken care of myself. I can go on. God, forgive me. Let me live.

Cold spread through her limbs. She rolled to her side and sat up. I must move, she realized, or I'll die after all.

Somehow she'd managed to hold onto her stick all through the tumble. Digging it into the snow, she heaved herself to her feet and turned to look back up the hill. She'd slid a long way. The rising moon shone on the wide swath she'd made through the deep snow.

A wry laugh rose up in her. That's one way to get down.

But the rest of the descent was difficult. In her collision with the boulder, she'd twisted her pelvis, and her legs were now hard to control. She wove and stumbled. In some part of her dimming mind, she recognized the symptoms of hypothermia. A bolt of fear shot through her, and the same fierce determination that had taken her up the ridge to die now rallied her to live. She picked up her pace.

Jabbing her stick in front of her, staggering around it, half running, she finally reached the bottom of the ridge and the trail around the lake. The relief of coming to level ground was soon overwhelmed by the realization that her legs were so wobbly and painful she could barely stand. She was trembling with cold. Her face was numb, and every breath felt like shards of ice piercing her lungs. Her consciousness wavered in and out of grayness. Her knees began to fold.

With a jolt, she pulled herself up. Clinging to her stick, she gazed at the long loop of trail, barely visible in the dimness, that led to the trailhead and her car. Still far away.

But not far at all if she cut across the frozen lake. In all the winters she'd walked there, she'd never tried that, always wary of treacherous ice. But it had been below zero last night and this one. Surely it was safe.

A waist-high rail fence separated the trail from the marshlands that spread out from the lake. Two years ago she would have just swung her long leg over it, hardly breaking her stride; but now it presented a formidable obstacle. She managed to hoist herself up to sit on the top rail, then rolled off to fall in the soft snow on the other side.

The snow was deeper there. She floundered through it over the frozen marshlands and came to the edge of the lake. There was almost no snow on its surface. The ice shone silver in the moonlight.

She stepped out onto the lake. It was much easier walking. She gave a sigh of relief. I'll make it, she thought, imagining her warm apartment. She planned a hot bath as soon as she got home. She walked on, more quickly.

A dull cracking sound reverberated through the ice. She stopped, rigid. All was still. She remembered the lake as she had seen it on her walk a few days ago. It had been mostly frozen, but a few ducks had been swimming in an area of open water. Her gut clenched as she realized she was standing on that part of the lake.

Carefully, warily, moving as slowly as the moon rises, she shifted a foot, moved a leg, and stepped back.

Another crack, then another. The ice wobbled under her feet. In panic, abandoning all caution, she scrambled backwards. The ice snapped, broke, and dropped her into black, frigid water.

She struggled, but only briefly. Already deeply chilled and exhausted, she didn't have a chance.

The waning moon glinted off the jagged shards that jutted up around the open water. For a few moments moonlight sparkled where the water rippled, then the ripples were still. A light wind sent scurries of snow across the ice and into the dark hole.

Chapter 2

Sunrise

Dawn awakened the colors and contours of the earth. In the growing light, the snowy peaks of the foothills, with their dark rocky faces, emerged against a blue-gray sky.

Harriet's consciousness floated up from a well of deep dreams and haunting, unearthly singing. With no memory of how she got there, she found herself standing at the top of the ridge, looking out to the east. She could still hear the singing within and around her, only now more clearly, a song of almost unbearable beauty, resonant with overtones and exquisite harmonies, like nothing she had ever heard or imagined. She realized she was singing, too, singing as she had never sung before, her voice blending with the others.

To the east and south, the low clouds were suffused with pink glow, burnished with orange.

The song grew stronger, fuller, vibrating through every cell of her body. She raised her arms and, as if in response, the first bright arc of the sun cleared the horizon. Still deeper and stronger, the song swelled until Harriet felt that the song and the sunrise were one and she was one with all creation.

Slowly, slowly the full orb of the sun freed itself from earth and floated low in the eastern sky, sending its golden light across the snow-covered hills and meadows below her, across the frozen lake and the city just awakening.

The song softened. The other voices began to fade, and her own song ended. There had been no words, only the glory, but now …

Did she imagine it? As the last traces of melody floated away, there were words singing within her. *Farewell, Harriet. Farewell. Our love is with you always.*

Then the voices were gone, leaving her with a sense of inconsolable loss.

She drew in a deep breath. The air was cold, sharp in her nostrils. She put her hands to her face to wipe away the tears that had been streaming down all the time she sang, and found that her cheeks were warm, as if she had not been in the cold for long.

Still vibrating with the intensity of the song and the sunrise, she took a few steps from the place where she had been standing and sank down on a flat rock sticking up out of the snow.

"What was that?" she whispered into the silent morning. "What was that?"

She'd always loved to sing, had sung in the church choir in her home town all through her teens, and later when she returned for visits. She had a sweet, clear voice, but never had she sung like that. Never such a song. Never such voices singing with her.

She turned on the rock and looked around her. A few evergreens draped in snow stood silent nearby.

There was no one there.

"But I didn't sing alone," she said to the rocks and trees. "Did you hear? Did you hear the other voices?"

The trees and rocks did not answer.

She looked down. The snow was deep, above her ankles. She could see her footprints from the place where she had been standing leading to the rock where she sat. There were no other footprints.

She stood, turned, and looked behind herself, then at the ridge path below her. For a moment she had the crazy notion she was disembodied. She took a few steps and looked down. Yes, she made footprints. But except for the few prints she had just made, the snow lay white and unbroken all around her.

She felt weak, suddenly cold, hungry, shaken. "How could—?" She looked around again. "Come on," she said, speaking aloud, impatient, frightened. "How did I get here without footprints? I didn't just drop out of heaven."

The trees, if they knew, were not telling.

She didn't remember coming there.

Hunching her shoulders against the cold, she tried to recall. But the only memories that came, first in shreds, then full on, were memories of the bitter walk in the night, the pain, the despair, the ethereal beauty of the moonrise, her tumble down the hillside, the ice breaking …

She wrapped her arms around herself. I was dying, she thought. Did I die? Was the singing heaven? Were the voices angels?

The hillside below her, the lake, the trail around the lake where she had walked so often, clear now in the morning sunlight, all looked everyday and familiar.

A gust of wind swirled the light snow around her feet and froze the remains of tears on her cheeks. Her practical side arose.

"Well, I don't know how I got here," she said aloud, "but I do know it's cold. And if the lake and the trail are there, probably my car is, too. And my warm apartment."

She looked around for her stick. No sign of it. As she took a step, another shock ran through her. Her leg. It didn't hurt anymore. She picked up her foot, swung her leg around. No pain. She stood still a moment, arrested by astonishment, then slowly bent forward, easily, freely. Stretched up and arched back. Still no pain. Before, if she'd even started such a movement, she'd have been stabbed by excruciating fire.

Unbelieving, warily, she began moving around, stepping, swinging her leg, bending her knees. She tried a little jump.

"Whoa!" she breathed. Then she dropped down on the rock and burst into tears. All the misery and desperation of the last two years poured out through her sobs. Could the pain really be gone? "Oh, my

God!" she exclaimed. Then exclamation became prayer. "Oh, my God, thank you."

Gradually she calmed, quieted her breath. She stood and began walking down the ridge path, making the first footprints in the untouched snow. No need for her stick. She walked in wonder, balancing easily, knees bending painlessly.

Where *is* my stick? she asked herself. At the bottom of the lake? No, that was a dream, a nightmare. It must have been, because at the end I was dying. And here I am, not only alive, but—

She stopped walking. The singing. Was that what had healed her? As if in answer to her thoughts, a wisp of sweet, strange melody flowed through her. She heard it not with her ears, but within. It was a wisp only, but of the same quality as the sunrise song. She remembered how that song had vibrated inside her, rocking her cells, penetrating her with intense, pulsing warmth.

Could a song heal? The melody within her grew stronger, and she felt a rush of energy. Then complete disorientation. As if the ground was shifting out from under her feet, the whole ridge tilting.

Just below her was the little hollow on the brink of which she had wavered in her dream, watching the moon rise.

As she approached, she saw footprints. They left the trail and went up to the hollow. Footprints coming back. Hers. She knew they were hers, but still she put her boot beside one of them, pressed it in and drew it back. Yes, they matched.

The footprints weren't fresh. A little snow had blown into them and the edges were slightly blurred.

She found she was holding her breath. She let it out slowly. Then it wasn't a nightmare. It had really happened. When? How long ago? It couldn't have been last night or the footprints would be fresher.

Perhaps what she was experiencing now was a dream. It felt as if it could be as she followed her footprints down the path, past the swath in the deep snow where she had slid and tumbled. She came to the trail at the foot of the ridge and found the place where she had rolled off the fence. She saw the single line of footprints leading to the lake, and, partway across the ice, the hole of black water.

A lone duck paddled there.

Cold shock knotted in her belly as she remembered the ice cracking, the dark water engulfing her, the futility of her struggle. Another memory, vague, fleeting. Hands gripping her shoulders.

Someone had pulled her out. But then why had she regained consciousness standing on the hillside singing instead of in the emergency room?

She glanced over the meadow between the fence and the lake. Only one line of footprints. Maybe her rescuer had come from the other side of the lake. But who could have found her in the dead of night? It made no sense.

Shaking her head from side to side, Harriet turned away from the lake and hurried around the trail to the parking lot. Her car was there. She fumbled in her pocket for the keys.

Chapter 3

Tiger

*H*er apartment was dim and chilly. Harriet took off her boots and coat and hurried around opening the blinds, turning up the heat, starting the coffee brewing. Being back in her own space, with the low grumble of the furnace, the smell of coffee, the African violet on the window sill began to restore her sense of reality. As she busied herself preparing breakfast, she let herself forget all the bewildering events of the morning. Soon she was settled at the little table in her breakfast nook, sipping her coffee and hungrily devouring fruit and yogurt, toast and eggs.

When she had finished eating and cleaning up, she went to her study and was jolted out of her temporary calm. On the desk was her suicide note. She picked it up.

"To all my loved ones," she had written. "I am sorry to leave you so abruptly, but I can no longer bear the pain in my body and in my heart. Farewell, Harriet."

Harriet lifted her head. A quiver ran through her. "Farewell, Harriet." That was what they had sung, the voices that sang with her that morning. Those same words that she had written in bitter grief had been full of love and beauty, drifting to her as the song faded away.

She looked down again at the suicide note in her hand. The writing, though legible, was jagged, scrawled on a blank sheet from her printer. She remembered how painful it had been to bend over the desk to write it, how desperate she had been in that moment, after sleepless hours unable to find any position in her bed that was bearable. After months of sleepless, pain-racked nights. After the ordeal of two spine surgeries that had given no relief, no hope.

She crumpled the paper in a quick, fierce motion and tossed it into the wastebasket.

What was I thinking? she asked herself. Who would have found this note? She had no children to come looking for her. Her ex-husband wouldn't be bothered. Her sisters and parents lived hours away.

Probably it would have been Brenda who found the note. Faithful Brenda, who would miss her when she didn't come to work and would be intrepid enough to break in when she didn't answer her phone or doorbell. Brenda, who loved her.

Harriet pressed her lips together, burning with shame. It would have been horrible for Brenda. And Brenda would never have known, no one would have known, that she'd changed her mind. Because then she fell through the ice and would have died after all if ...

Her thoughts ran smack into a wall.

What had happened?

She turned away from her desk and paced the small room. Her sense of reality went askew again, folded, layers overlapping, sliding into patterns that had nothing to do with the three dimensional reality she knew. The singing—so strange and yet so beautiful. And she'd been part of it, singing with the unseen voices, swept away into a glory like light streaming down from the high arc of heaven. Never had she known such a feeling, so connected, so wrapped in love.

She had paced into the kitchen and found herself clinging to the counter. She felt dizzy, almost nauseated, and at the same time wanted to weep with wonder. Her pain was gone! Blessing had come to her undeserved, to her who had almost thrown away the gift of life.

She took a long breath, returned to her study, and sank into her chair. Her calendar lay open on the desk beside her computer. She saw the names of the patients she was scheduled to see on Monday, January 16th.

Oh, no! Her stomach clenched. What day is it? How long have I been gone? Did I miss a day at work, stand up all my patients? It had been Friday night when she wrote the note and went out into the night to die. She remembered that. She also remembered that the footprints from that night had been blurred. Sucking in her breath, she tapped her keyboard. The computer screen lit up. There was the date—Sunday, January 15, 2012, 9:34 a.m.

She let out a sigh of relief. So, she thought, I left on Friday night and now it's Sunday morning, and I have no idea, *no idea*, where I've been for more than twenty-four hours. No idea how I came to be standing on the hillside singing, hearing other voices singing with me.

She realized then that the clothes she was wearing were the same ones she'd had on when she fell through the ice. They were dry. Then she remembered that even though it had probably been well below freezing that morning, her cheeks had been warm. Her cheeks wouldn't have been warm if she'd climbed the hill in the predawn cold. Anyway, there had been no footprints.

Her mind tilted again, careening around those impossible perceptions. I'm losing my marbles, she thought. More than twenty-four hours and I can't remember anything. I'm too young to be losing my memory.

She got up from the desk and paced again. It was a modest condo, only a living room with kitchenette, two bedrooms and a bath, but it was hers. She'd purchased it with the money from Jared when he bought her out of the elegant house they'd shared for twenty years. She loved her condo; it was home, but it was small. Not much room for pacing for a long-legged woman like her.

I need to go out, she thought. Walk. I want to go back to the lake and go all around it to see if I can find any sign of my rescuers.

As she bent to put on her boots, a wave of jubilation swept through her. No pain! Then tears rushed to her eyes. *Thank you, thank you,* she prayed to her unknown healer. A wisp of song moved through her, not heard but vibrating in her cells, and with it the same strange rush of energy that she'd experienced earlier when walking down the ridge path.

She stood still a moment, feeling it. It *was* the singing that healed me, she realized. She didn't understand how, or how she knew, but was sure that was true.

When Harriet stepped outside, she saw her next-door neighbor, Leah, standing on her front porch. She was balancing a big box on one knee and struggling to reach her keys in the handbag slung over her shoulder.

Harriet had moved into her condo only three months before, and didn't know Leah very well, only that she was young and pale and worked as a bank teller. She slumped, her upper spine bent like a wind-battered tree, and her long, tangled, dyed-red hair hung half across her face. Harriet had slumped and hidden behind her own hair enough times to know what that meant. Even though she could tell that Leah was lonely, she'd felt too shy to reach out.

But now Leah was crying.

Harriet hurried across the narrow strip of lawn that separated their two porches. "Leah, what's wrong? Here, let me hold that for you." She took the big box out of Leah's arms. It was a cat crate. Harriet caught a glimpse of black and brown fur through the wire walls.

"It's Tiger," Leah explained through her sobs. "He's dying." She pressed her hand over her mouth and nose, then rubbed at her tears, leaving a streak of glistening mucous across her cheek. "The vet said … I should put him down." She paused to dig deeper into her handbag. "Because he's suffering … but I can't let him go … he's all I have."

Leah finally found her key and opened the door. "Can you help me?" she asked.

"Of course. What can I do?"

They went into Leah's condo, the mirror image of Harriet's, except that Leah's was a mess—dirty dishes piled in the kitchenette, magazines, papers, clothes scattered over the floor and couch.

"Just stay with him. I don't want to leave him alone." Leah rubbed the tears on her cheeks again and pushed back her hair. "But I've gotta go get his medicine. When I wouldn't let the vet put him to sleep, he gave me this prescription, so Tiger wouldn't hurt so much."

"How about I go get the prescription?" Harriet suggested. "Then you can stay with him."

"No. I have to use my credit card—it would be too complicated." Leah pulled a tissue out of her pocket and blew her nose. "Just stay with him. Please."

"I really think it would be better—" Harriet began. But Leah was already at the door.

"I'll just go grab his medicine and be back real quick."

The door closed behind her.

Harriet was still holding the cat crate. She set it on the end of the couch, pushed aside some magazines, sat down beside the crate, and opened it.

The cat did not look good. His fur was dull and matted, his eyes dim. When she bent down to look closer, he stretched a paw out toward her and let out a husky meow.

Harriet had grown up with pets and was especially fond of cats. "Poor Tiger," she said. "You're having a tough time. Would you like to come out and sit in my lap?"

Carefully supporting his head and hindquarters, she slid her hands under him and lifted him into her lap. He was stiff and smelled rank.

"Poor kitty." Harriet ran her hand gently along his body. As soon as she touched him, the same strange energy of the inner melody vibrated inside her again. There was a swelling in her chest. Then song poured out of her, wild, sweet, uncontainable. Frightened, she held her breath, but the pressure of the song was too great. With her next exhale, it poured out again, not only out of her mouth, but also out of her hand where it rested lightly on Tiger's belly.

Such a song. Strange sounds like words, but no words of any earthly language; deep, full sounds with overtones, as wondrous and beautiful as the song she had sung at sunrise, only now she sang alone.

Looking down, Harriet could see *into Tiger's body*, could *see* the tumor pressing all his abdominal organs aside. She gasped, but could not stop singing. The song rose and swelled and power flowed through her hand into Tiger. As she watched with the miraculous, new sight that could see inside him, she saw the tumor shrink, then dissolve, and the organs begin shifting back into what she instinctively knew were their proper places. Her hand moved, guided by the song, and she found more tumors, infection, a twist in his spine.

She sang, vibrating with the light that flowed through the song, through her hand. As she sang, she saw the tumors dissolve, the infection clear, the spine straighten. Tiger gave a long sigh, stretched and softened. The song faded.

Harriet came back from far away to winter sunlight slanting across the untidy room and the low rumble of Tiger's purr.

He was warm in her lap and the rank smell was gone. Harriet stroked him. Already his fur felt better. She trembled, tears welling up in her eyes, too awed to question.

She only knew that the song healed. It had healed her and now, through her, it had healed Tiger. She could hear remnants of it vibrating through her cells, a fragment of melody drifting in her heart.

She looked down at her hand resting on Tiger's side. She couldn't see inside him anymore. That strange sight had ended with the song.

She shivered.

As if in response to her fear, melody swelled within her. *Ah*, it seemed to sing, and she was washed with a wave of compassion.

Then she was singing aloud again, softly, a gentle song. There were no words, yet she heard the song soothing her, telling her not to be frightened, she had done well, they were with her, they loved her.

They? She sang and was comforted in spite of her questions.

The door banged open. The song ended. Leah dropped her bag and package on the floor, shrugged out of her coat and dropped that, too.

"You were singing," she said. "I heard you as I came in. That was the prettiest song. I didn't know you could sing." Leah came over and looked at Tiger. "How is he? He's so still ..."

"He's sleeping," Harriet assured her. "See his breath moving?"

"Oh." Leah stroked him. "Were you singing to him?"

"Yes." Harriet didn't know what to say, still reeling from her strange experience. "He ... he seemed to like it."

"Cool. Could you help me a little more, hold him while I stick his pills down his throat? He hates that and always gives me a hard time."

As if she were Tiger, Harriet recoiled.

"Maybe you should wait," she suggested. "He's sleeping now and seems peaceful."

Leah stroked her cat. "He does. Okay, I'll wait."

"Where shall I put him?" Harriet asked.

"On my bed."

Harriet gathered up the sleeping cat and followed Leah into the bedroom. As she laid him down on the rumpled quilt, he purred briefly, then slept again.

⁐ ⁌

Harriet sat curled up in the corner of her couch with a cup of tea, struggling to make sense of her day. It was 5:30, already dark.

After she left Leah and Tiger, she had spent several hours walking around the lake, approaching its edge from every angle, walking back up the ridge trail. Finally, cold and tired, she had come home none the wiser.

Even with all the walking, her leg had not hurt. Not at all. When she lay down to rest, she slept deeply and woke stretched out on her back. She hadn't been able to sleep on her back for two years without setting off unbearable fire down her leg. She'd lain on her bed awhile, hardly believing that she could rest like that, breathing gratitude.

And now, curled on her couch, still no pain. She took another sip of tea.

I have to figure this out, she told herself. Maybe if I write it all down … She got up and found a pad and pencil, then settled back on the couch and wrote:

1. I was rescued from an icy death. By whom? No clue.
2. The sciatica that tormented me for two years and finally drove me to attempted suicide is gone, healed.
3. I woke up from twenty-four hours I don't remember, standing on the hillside, singing the most incredible song of my life, with no footprints to show how I got there. Singing with other voices. But no one was there.
4. I know it was the singing that healed me. How do I know that?
5. Somehow the song got inside me and healed Tiger.
6. It seemed as if the voices sang to me afterward, telling me not to be afraid.

Nothing made sense.

Maybe I'm going crazy, she thought. Maybe I'm hallucinating and nothing really happened with the cat. Or maybe this is all a dream. Dreams can be like this.

She remembered hearing somewhere that if she were dreaming, she wouldn't have a reflection in the mirror.

She set down her tea cup and went to the bathroom. The mirror did show a reflection. My hair's a mess, she thought, impatiently rumpling her short, straight hair. Well, if it's a dream, the mirror is part of it.

She started to turn away, then turned back. Her eyes were different. She leaned closer to look at them. They had always been a sort of murky green, an unattractive mix of her mother's blue eyes and her father's brown ones. They were still green, but now a deep, clear green with flecks of gold. And they were bigger, set wider in her face and slightly turned up at the corners. They were beautiful.

Nothing about Harriet, in Harriet's opinion, had ever been beautiful. Except maybe her hair, long ago, when it had hung thick, deep brown, and shining to her waist.

The mirror blurred and for a brief flash, she thought she saw other eyes shaped as hers were now, unfathomable, luminous eyes full of compassion and ancient wisdom.

She gripped the edge of the washbasin. Stop it, she told herself. You're making things up. She looked back at the mirror and saw her own face again, but her eyes were still strange. She felt shaky as she hurried out of the bathroom.

I know, I'll call the police. They'd have a record if someone was pulled out of the lake.

Her hands still shook as she thumbed through the phone book. She called the police, then the hospital. There was no record of anyone being pulled out of the lake, only one case of hypothermia on Friday night, a homeless man.

She was standing by her desk, the phone still in her hand, when she heard a knock on the door. It was Leah, bursting with excitement.

"Tiger's better!" she exclaimed. "When I went to check on him, a while after you left, he was sitting up and washing himself. Then he came to the kitchen and ate everything in his dish, and drank his water, and meowed for more food. And he's been playing, chasing his ball. And just now he jumped up on the counter. He hasn't been able to do that for months."

I knew he was healed, Harriet thought, but I couldn't really believe it. "That's wonderful," she managed to say.

Leah was waving a pill bottle in her hand. "I came to see if you would help me give him his pills, but now I don't know if I should, since he's better. You're a doctor, aren't you? Maybe you can tell me what's in them and if I should still give them to him now he's better."

Harriet took the pill bottle and studied the label. "I'm not a medical doctor, you know. I'm a chiropractor. But I know this drug. It's pretty strong and can have serious side effects. Okay for a dying cat, but I wouldn't give it to him now."

"A chiropractor? Did you crack his bones or anything?"

"No," Harriet said carefully.

Leah tilted her head, squinting her eyes a little as she regarded Harriet. "I just wondered, 'cause it seemed he got well while you were holding him."

Harriet was silent. She handed the pill bottle back to Leah.

Leah pushed her hair back and smiled at Harriet. "Thanks for the info about the pills. I don't want him to have side effects. I think I'll take them back, get a plus on my credit card." She dropped the bottle into a pocket of her cargo pants.

As she went out the door, she said over her shoulder, "Maybe it was that pretty song you were singing."

Harriet leaned back against the closed door, fear contracting her belly. How did Leah even guess it was her singing that had healed Tiger? It was all too weird.

She slid slowly down the door until she was hunched on the floor, her head on her knees. "Oh, God," she whispered. "What's happening to me?"

Chapter 4

Monday

*H*arriet's office was on the end of a row of one-story offices in a small strip mall in the old part of Boulder. She had chosen it because it was full of light with windows on three sides and a little lawn with a tree in front.

At eight forty-five on Monday morning, Harriet sat in her car in the parking place behind her office, twisting her key chain around her fingers. Her stomach was queasy. What if the Song came again? (She'd started thinking of it with a capital S to distinguish it from other songs.) What if she started singing as soon as she touched her first patient? What if her patients went out and told everyone? In the flip of a coin she'd go from being a respectable chiropractor to another one of Boulder's weirdos.

She glanced at her watch and sucked in her breath. Five of nine. Her first patient would be arriving any minute. She gathered herself, opened the car door, and swung her long legs out.

Winter sun slanted through the south windows of the waiting room, brightening the rich brown of the carpet, the deep green of the ivy on the bookshelf. Brenda looked up from her desk with a wide, warm smile. "Hi, honey. Happy Monday."

Harriet loved Brenda's smile. She felt a twist of guilt about her attempted suicide, then a rush of gratitude that she was alive and the suicide note was destroyed. What if she had died and never seen Brenda again?

"Happy Monday yourself," Harriet replied, returning her smile.

"You look good," Brenda said.

Harriet hung up her coat on the coat tree beside Brenda's black leather jacket and bent to take off her boots, already used to how easy it was.

Brenda pushed her chair back and stared at Harriet across her desk. "Whoa!" she exclaimed, "you look *really* good. Moving around so easily. Taking off your boots without even sitting down. Where's your cane?"

"I don't know. I don't need it anymore."

Brenda scooted out from behind her desk, hurried up to Harriet, and put her plump hands on either side of Harriet's face. "What happened to you? You look fabulous."

"I slept well last night," Harriet said.

That was an understatement. She had slept deeply, turning as she needed to without pain, and waked stretched out on her back, soft and relaxed. Such a blessing!

The bell over the door rang and Harriet's first patient came in.

"Good morning, Celia," Harriet said. "I'll be with you in just a moment. Come with me," she said to Brenda, led her into the treatment room, and closed the door. "I need to talk to you. I've had an amazing weekend. If I didn't feel so great, I'd think I'd gone nuts. But my pain is gone. I'm healed."

"I can see that." Brenda had tears in her eyes. "How did it happen, all at once, after all you've tried?"

"I'll tell you, but Celia's here and I need to get to work. What's my schedule like today?"

"You're full this morning—six patients—but there's a cancellation at one."

"Perfect. Then we can have a longer lunch break."

"I can't wait to hear what happened. I'm so glad. You look beautiful, like yourself again."

Harriet hugged her, resting her cheek against the top of Brenda's head. "I never was beautiful, you know that. But I do feel years younger without the pain." Harriet squeezed Brenda tighter. "Thank you, Brenda."

"It wasn't me that fixed you. What're you thanking me for?"

"For being you."

"Humph. Shall I send that Celia in?"

"I guess it's time. But give me just a minute more."

After Brenda closed the door behind her, Harriet sat on the edge of her treatment table, rubbing her brow. Celia. What if the Song did come and was able to completely heal Celia? Like it did Tiger.

She'd seen him that morning chasing a squirrel up the tree in front of her building, his coat sleek and shining, his tail lashing. He was clearly fine.

In a rush of images, Harriet saw all the patients whose chronic miseries persisted in spite of her best efforts. What if the Song could completely heal all of them? Like a startled bird taking wing, hope fluttered up in her heart.

Celia, a frowzy, middle-aged woman, was one of her more frustrating patients. As far as Harriet could tell, there wasn't much wrong with her, but she was a stellar whiner. She came three times a week with headaches, back pain, plus myriad other symptoms that came and went. Harriet never thought she was doing her much good and felt guilty for taking her money. She'd consoled herself by thinking maybe it did Celia good to just get some attention.

Anyway, there she was out in the waiting room and Harriet was already five minutes late. She opened the door and called her in.

The moment Harriet laid her hands on Celia's shoulders, the Song rose in her. Quickly, she pulled her hands away. The Song quieted. But I have to touch her, Harriet thought desperately. Slowly, carefully, she put her hands back on Celia's shoulders. The Song rose in her again. She jerked with a sudden tremor and let out an odd squeak, but managed not to make any other sound. The Song was energy flowing through her hands. She could hear its beauty singing within her and realized, with a shiver of relief, that she wasn't singing aloud. Then she felt the Song guiding her, as it had with Tiger. Her inside-the-body vision opened. Chills ran through her as she studied Celia's neck. It was as she had thought it would be from all the times she'd manipulated it, except for one thing. Celia's first rib was turned. Harriet had never caught that. It would be enough to cause a headache.

She went to work, holding the power of the Song silent, moving into a kind of trance as she straightened the rib, derotated the first thoracic vertebra, then worked up and down the entire spine from cranium to tail bone. She finished with a sigh that became a hum.

Celia sat up. "I feel good," she said in surprise. She'd never said that before, only complained about some other symptom.

As Harriet helped her down from the table, she felt a rush of tenderness for this woman she had been treating for years. The Song is love, she realized. I cannot sing it, even silently, without loving the person I sing to. Perhaps it is the love that heals.

Then she felt shame for all the times she'd been impatient with Celia, for the unkind remarks she'd made about her to Brenda. No wonder Celia didn't heal.

There were five more patients after Celia, all of them ones Harriet had treated many times. With each one, she grew more skillful in holding the Song silent, though at times odd hums escaped her. The Song was light and power pouring through her. It guided her hands to unexpected places. She knew by the time she'd completed her half-hour session with each of them that a miracle had happened, and the Song had resolved all their difficulties.

It was overwhelming. She had to hold back tears of awe and love after each one left and pull herself together to meet the next.

At last, it was noon and time for lunch with Brenda.

Brenda had been her best friend and confidant ever since Harriet first arrived in Denver, fresh out of chiropractic school, young, heartbroken, and scared of the big city. It had been Brenda's warm smile that welcomed her the first day she walked into Reilly's Chiropractic where Brenda was office manager. Although she was married with two small children, Brenda was only six years older than Harriet. During the three years Harriet was part of that practice, they became close friends; and when Eliza Reilly became disillusioned with her work and closed her practice, Brenda had moved her family up to Boulder to help Harriet open her new office.

Over all the years, twenty-nine of them now, Brenda had been there, keeping the office running smoothly, providing myriad little details of support each day. Harriet treasured her warm presence, her irreverent humor, her love.

By the time Harriet had finished with her last patient of the morning, Brenda had the tea kettle on and their lunches laid out on the table in the little private room behind the waiting room.

As soon as they were settled, Brenda said, "Now tell me. What miracle happened for you? I've been watching you move around. I can't believe what I see. And your face is so—I don't know. You're shining, and your eyes … There's something different about your eyes."

"Oh." Harriet bent her head and covered her eyes with her hand, embarrassed.

She'd studied her face in the mirror again that morning. Her eyes were bigger than they'd been before, but fit in okay with her strong jaw and large nose. They were beautiful, striking, their color clear and deep. Still, there was something almost inhuman about their shape that made her shiver. How could her eyes have changed like that? She'd hoped no one would notice. But, of course, Brenda would.

After a moment she moved her hand. "I don't know how to tell you, how to begin. I feel like I've gone nuts. Or maybe … It's all confused."

"Start at the beginning."

"The beginning. Okay. Friday night I tried to kill myself."

"*What?* Oh, honey, was it that bad? You should have called me."

Brenda's distress exacerbated Harriet's guilt. She plunged on. "But I didn't die. As you see. I changed my mind. But then it was too late, and I would have died anyway except that someone rescued me, I don't know who. And now I'm healed. . . And there's more."

"Slow down. Tell me everything. In order."

So Harriet told her about the walk up the hill in the cold night. Brenda listened, leaning forward over the table on her elbows, interrupting from time to time to better understand.

"Why did you change your mind?"

"Because of the stars. And the moonrise. It was so beautiful. I couldn't bear to let it go, and die. I didn't know what would happen after. Maybe there would be no stars."

"Yeah. It's pretty mysterious, what happens after. Go on."

When Harriet told how she had fallen through the ice, Brenda gasped. "How did you get out?"

"That's what I don't know. I have no clue."

"You don't know?"

"No. I don't remember anything before yesterday morning." Harriet went on to tell Brenda about standing on the hillside, singing to the sunrise with strange, unearthly voices all around her, warm and dry, the pain gone, no footprints until she reached the hollow where she had intended to die, the marks in the snow and the hole in the ice confirming that it had all really happened.

Brenda listened with her mouth hanging open.

"And it was Sunday morning, yesterday, when I got home ... and found my suicide note ... and I have no memory of anything between falling through the ice and singing the sun up. More than twenty-four hours blank."

"But whatever happened in that time healed your pain?

"There's more. I haven't told you about Tiger."

"Tiger?"

"My neighbor's cat."

Harriet told Brenda about the Song healing the cat. "Then today, this morning," she went on, "I was pretty worried I'd just start singing. It's beautiful, the Song, but strange, really strange, like nothing I ever heard before, much less heard coming out of my own mouth. I was afraid my patients would freak out, so somehow I figured out how to keep it silent and still let it do its work. And it did. I feel pretty certain it healed everything that was wrong with the six people I saw this morning. They won't need to come back. If I keep this up, I won't have a practice left. But I can't not. I want them all to be well."

Brenda put her hand over her ample bosom. "Oh, my God! You've been doing that just on the other side of the door all morning? But I felt it. Something different, and then you coming out with your face all shiny. Don't you worry about your practice folding. If you really did those folks up like you say, even if they don't need to come back, the word will be out and we'll be swamped."

Harriet felt a chill of foreboding. "I didn't think of that."

"Oh, my God." Brenda shook her head. "We'll be swamped for sure. Honey, we've been busy enough. Even before this. A long waiting list. Folks love you for your skill and your big heart.

"But never mind all that. I need to know, *why did you try to kill yourself?* Was it the pain, the divorce? What made you so desperate as to do that?"

Harriet struggled with her guilt. "It was wrong of me. Sinful really, like they say in church. Yes, it was the pain—that had become unbearable—and the divorce. Then Friday afternoon Anna Martin came in with her newborn. I held him for a few minutes and he looked up at me with those deep, dreamy eyes that newborns have, and it just broke my heart that I'd never have children of my own. Even after Jared gave his ultimatum, I still had a grain of hope that maybe the birth control would fail. But that never happened. And now I'm into menopause and he's gone. I know I'm better off without him, who he has become."

"You sure are, the soulless bastard."

"But it still really hurts. I thought I'd be over it by now. It's been three months."

"Honey, it takes a while. Three months isn't long enough for stuff like that. It took me years to get over my Mick walking out on me."

Harriet remembered vividly what Brenda had done when her husband left. She'd bought a motorcycle, affectionately named it "Hog," and had a snake tattooed around her left upper arm. A more life-affirming choice than suicide. Harriet appreciated that Brenda, in spite of her inner wildness, had always maintained a respectable image in the office. She confined her unruly gray hair in a bun and after the tattoo, had taken to wearing long sleeves so her snake wouldn't upset Harriet's more conservative clientele. Harriet still felt an inward chuckle at the incongruity of her plump, matronly-looking office manager roaring off on her Harley at the end of the work day.

"It took you years, really?" Harriet asked. "I don't want to hear that. I'll get over it sooner. I'm angry. He defeminized me. No children. And he insisted I cut my hair, the only thing I thought was pretty about me. Remember my hair?"

"It was gorgeous. But you look good in that classy cut you have now. Only you need a trim."

Harriet pushed back her hair. "I know. I've been putting it off, thinking I might want to grow my hair out again. But it won't be the same. It's graying now."

She turned her head away and pressed her lips together. She remembered Neal running his fingers through her long, shining hair, burying his face in it as he lay over her. She'd never told anyone about Neal. Not even Brenda.

She took a breath. "Anyway," she said, "it all piled up on Friday. The pain was extra bad, I couldn't sleep because of it. I saw my surgeon last Wednesday and he said we'd have to fuse the spine. I couldn't face another surgery, especially since I had no hope it would make any difference. And I felt so alone. No husband, no kids. What's the use of going on? No one needs me."

"Tell that to the fifty-plus patients who count on you to keep them going."

"But Brenda, I didn't think I could work much longer. It hurt so much to bend over the table. Then—nothing to live for."

"Aw, Harriet, I sure wish I'd known how bad it was for you. You call me if you ever get down like that again, you hear? I don't want you disappearing on me."

"I won't do it again. It was wrong, I know. Life is a gift we shouldn't throw away. I felt really awful when I realized it would probably have been you who found my note. But what do you think of the rest of my story? It's so strange, I feel like I'm dreaming. Or hallucinating. Do you have any ideas about how I got out of the lake? And the pain going away? And the Song?"

"How you got out of that lake," Brenda said, "I've no clue. Or how you found yourself singing on the hillside without footprints. But I've been watching you all morning moving around like nothing hurts. Seeing your patients coming in limping and walking out easy. And you with your face all shiny like you had a light on inside of you. Looks to me like some kind of miracle happened. I don't understand it, but I'm pretty sure it's real."

Harriet shook her head in bewilderment. "How could it be?"

Brenda ate some of her salad and pushed Harriet's sandwich closer to her.

"Maybe," she said, "going through that near death experience, being in the ice water and all, changed something in your brain that made the pain go away and made you psychic, so you could see inside your patients and see how to fix them."

"Maybe." Harriet frowned and bit her lower lip. "But that still doesn't explain how I got out of the lake and, twenty-four hours later, up on the ridge with no footprints. Singing."

Brenda sighed and shook her head. "Eat, honey," she said. "You haven't touched your food. Time's moving on. You don't want to go into the afternoon on an empty stomach."

"You're right." Harriet realized she was hungry and picked up her sandwich. They ate awhile in silence.

Then Brenda tilted her head and looked across at Harriet. "If we believed in angels," she said, "that would solve everything. They were watching over you. Maybe they helped you change your mind. Then when you fell through the ice, they pulled you out, took you to heaven and fixed you up. Knowing the work you do and having compassion for the suffering of humankind, they gave you the Song and sent you back to heal. They had wings, so they could just set you down on the hill and sing with you. That's why no footprints. Why you were warm and dry. That explains everything."

"It does," Harriet said, "except that I don't believe in angels." She hesitated, remembering the voices singing with her, the heavenly beauty of the Song. "At least, I don't think I do."

"Another possibility." Brenda took a bite of her salad, and then went on. "Aliens. You were abducted by aliens. Same story as with the angels, except they took you up in their spaceship, brought you back, dropped you on the hill. Good aliens, not the monsters they scare you with in the movies."

"You know there's no such thing as aliens."

"There's plenty of folks that think there are. Never mind. I'm just making things up. But what's important is not what happened last weekend, especially since we can't figure it out, but what you're gonna do about it today. And I'm guessing that when Frank comes in at 1:30, he's gonna come in limping and walk out smooth. Now you'd better get going, honey. It's 1:25."

Later that afternoon, when Harriet came out to greet her 4:30 patient, Brenda beckoned to her. "I just got a call from a man real upset. His boy ran into a tree skiing and is all messed up. They've been to the hospital and had x-rays. No broken bones, but the kid's in a lot of pain. Someone gave the dad your name, and he's begging for you to see his boy today. What do you think about putting him in at five?"

Harriet hesitated. She was both weary and exhilarated from having the Song moving through her all day. But a child … "How old is the boy?"

"Eight, the dad said."

"Only eight? Oh. Tell them to come."

"You sure? You've had a long day."

"I'll be okay."

The child who showed up at five was small and skinny, pale under his freckles. His father carried him in. "It hurts him to walk," he explained. Harriet could see the man was struggling to hold back tears. The boy was silent, tense in his father's arms, his jaw clenched, his eyes unfocused.

Harriet's heart ached. All the tenderness she'd hoped to give the children she'd never have flowed out to the boy. "Lay him here," she told the father.

His small body covered less than half the table.

"What's your name?" she asked the boy.

"Jack."

"Okay, Jack. I'm going to put my hands on you gently to see where you are hurt. Is that okay?"

The boy nodded.

As soon as Harriet touched him, the Song swelled up in her stronger than it had all day. Her vision opened. The child was indeed in bad shape, his spine twisted and compressed, his abdominal organs bruised and displaced, torn tendons around his knee, concussion. Too much trouble to keep the Song silent.

Harriet turned to the father. "Sometimes it helps the energy flow if I sing while I do the adjustments."

"Whatever works," the father said. The boy looked up at her.

She drew in her breath and released the Song.

Out in the waiting room, Brenda lifted her head and laid her hand over her heart. Her eyes widened, then filled with tears. "Oh, my," she breathed. "Maybe there *are* angels."

Chapter 5

Ecstasy and Chaos

That night Harriet dreamed. Huge, round bubbles glowing with soft, silver light floated around her. Her whole being was filled with their wild, sweet Song. She felt as if they were sending her messages, teaching her. In her dream, she understood, but when she woke the next morning, heart bursting with the heavenly love she felt from them and the unearthly beauty of their Song, the meaning had slipped away.

What can they be? she asked herself as she dressed and prepared for work. Bubbles of light? Is that what they look like, the ones who healed me and gave me the Song? *Could* they be angels? Who knows what angels really look like. Oh, I wish I could remember what they were telling me.

In her office, the morning went more easily than the day before. She began to gain confidence that she could work with the energy of the Song without singing out loud. She had always been able to focus well when doing her work, but also remain aware of the room around her and sounds coming from outside. Now when the Song rose in her and her sight into the body opened, she was swept away into another world entirely, enfolded in a cocoon of sound and vibration and wondrous love. At moments as she worked, she almost remembered the meaning given to her in the dream, but before she could catch it, it slipped away.

Her trance was broken when she came out of her treatment room to greet her last client of the morning. A tall, thin man with a hooked nose and a gray goatee stood in the waiting room. As she opened the door, he turned to her.

"Dr. Ellis?"

"Yes."

"My name is Joel Peterson. I'm from the *Daily Camera* and I'd like to have a few words with you."

Harriet glanced at her next client, Janet, with severe scoliosis, sitting in her usual chair.

"Only a few words. I have a patient waiting."

"Tell me what happened here yesterday with the boy named Jack. I've talked with his father and some of the medical staff at the hospital. This morning they repeated the MRIs and scans they did yesterday after his accident. All signs of the injury were gone, everything was normal. The father says it was because of your treatment of the boy. That it was a miracle. That you sang to him."

Harriet felt a rush of joy at the affirmation that Jack was indeed healed, then a chill of unease. The man was intimidating, looking intently at her through wire-rimmed glasses, pad and pen poised in his hands.

"Tell me what you did," he ordered. "Where did you learn to sing like that? The father said it was very strange."

Harriet stiffened. After thirty years of Jared's domination, she had little tolerance for being bossed around by men. She lifted her chin. "I don't discuss my patients' treatments due to doctor-patient confidentiality. Please excuse me. I'm running late. Come in, Janet." She whisked into her treatment room. As Janet followed more slowly, she heard Mr. Peterson addressing Brenda.

"What can you tell me about what happened here yesterday?"

"Mister, you heard Dr. Ellis about confidentiality. It's time for you to leave now."

Harriet closed the door. Good old Brenda.

At lunch, Brenda told her the phone had been ringing, and Harriet had several new patients. "Those ones you worked with yesterday have been talking to their friends," she said. "You're gonna be busy."

"I'm kind of worried about that reporter," Harriet said. "Even though we wouldn't tell him anything, he's talked to Jack's dad and the hospital staff."

Her worry was well founded. Wednesday morning there was a headline in the local paper, "Miraculous Healing Through Song," and a picture of Jack looking happy and well.

The rest of the week was chaotic. Brenda answered the phone all day, telling people that Dr. Ellis's practice was full, and they could be put on a waiting list. But some people would not be deterred and started coming to the office, crowding the waiting room for a chance to see Dr. Ellis, bringing sick and injured children, or sitting there saying they wanted to hear the Song. Brenda asked them politely to leave, told them Dr. Ellis did not sing out loud, but some insisted on seeing the doctor, and when Harriet emerged between patients, pressed around her.

Their interruptions got Harriet off schedule, which annoyed her, even as she was concerned for those who pleaded for her immediate attention. In between the interruptions, she would meet her next patient and enter the trance, lost in the Song and love for the person she was touching. Then out again into her crowded waiting room. The ecstasy of the Song pouring through her juxtaposed with her frustration at the chaos in her usually quiet and orderly office made her feel as if she were on a bungee cord, bouncing back and forth between irritation and bliss. She couldn't resist the children, so she ended her day on Wednesday fitting in three of them and working until eight o'clock.

Evenings at home, as she fixed her meal, bathed, and prepared for bed, she repeatedly found herself stopped in the middle of whatever she was doing, immobilized by the immensity of what was happening in her life. She had become so used to the pain, she hardly felt like herself without it, could barely believe the blessing of its absence. Was it true really? Would she wake any moment and find herself crippled again by the burning anguish in her leg? But no, she'd walked out into the night to end it, fallen through the ice— Then the impossibility of it all would leave her clinging dizzily to a sink or door frame.

When she slept, the bubbles floated around her, silvery, iridescent with color like soap bubbles in the sun, singing to her, explaining it all. All lost in the waking.

On Thursday, Harriet just stayed in her treatment room and had Brenda usher the next patient in. The only problem was that the bathroom was off the waiting room, so she went all morning without peeing. At noon Brenda somehow managed to clear everyone out, lock the door, and turn off the phone.

"You can't keep this up, honey," she said as she set out Harriet's lunch on the table in the back room. "No more adding people on at the end of the day. You do that and the word'll get out that they don't need an appointment, they can just come here and you'll take pity on them. You'll never get any rest."

"It was the children."

"Honey, you can't."

"What'll we do?"

"For now I'm keeping the door locked and only letting in those that have an appointment."

Friday morning, a woman squeezed in with the 11:30 patient. Except for a rainbow-striped scarf over her head and shoulders, she was dressed all in black, with a skirt down to her ankles. Long, straight black hair hung down on either side of her face, and her large brown eyes were heavily accented with mascara and eye shadow.

"I've heard," she said to Harriet in a low, husky voice, "that you are being visited by powerful benevolent beings from the other side of the veil. I'm a medium and can connect you with them."

She gave Harriet a long, soulful look and handed her a card. "Morna Morningstar," it said. "Séances, Life Readings."

Harriet drew in a deep breath, pressing back hysterical laughter. "Thank you," she said. "I don't feel in need of your services just now, but I appreciate you thinking of me. Please excuse me. I have a patient waiting."

Morna nodded and drifted out.

"Only in Boulder," Harriet muttered to Brenda as she passed her desk on the way to the treatment room.

During their lunch break, Harriet and Brenda had just started eating when they heard a pounding on the locked office door. Brenda got up, opened the door of the back room and peered out. "There's a couple out there, wanting in," she said.

Something inside Harriet snapped. She pushed back her chair and stood, clutching her throat. "Brenda, what can I do? There's a world of misery outside that locked door. I can't take care of everyone in pain. But I can't turn them away. I know what it's like to hurt. Why should I be the lucky one who got healed? I don't know what to do." Leaving her lunch on the table, she dashed into the waiting room and started putting on her coat.

Brenda was right behind her. "Wait a minute, honey. Where're you going?"

"I don't know. Out of here." Three long strides took her to the treatment room, trailing her coat, only one arm in the sleeve. She grabbed her purse out of her desk drawer. Three strides back to the waiting room. She twisted, struggling to find the second sleeve of her coat. "Tell that couple and the rest of the patients I've had a family emergency. That's it. I'll go down to my parents' place. No one will find me there. I don't know when I'll be back."

Brenda caught her arm. "Easy, honey. Is this really what you want to do?"

"I've just got to get away." Confusion, desperation, fear tumbled through her, constricting her chest, stopping all reasonable thought. She was still fighting with her coat.

Brenda lifted it and helped her slide her arm into the sleeve."Drive careful, then." She pulled Harriet close in a quick, warm hug. "Call me when you get there."

"Okay. Bye." Harriet opened the door. With a muttered "Excuse me," she pushed past the couple waiting there and ran around the building to where her car was parked in back.

Chapter 6

Flight

It wasn't the best time to be on the road—rush hour on a Friday afternoon and snowing. In a way the traffic and the snow were a blessing as they demanded all her focus, so there was no mental space left for thoughts. Route 36 to 270, through Denver to I-70, south and east.

She'd forgotten how abruptly the city ended on I-70. All at once the lights were behind her and, although she was still on the four-lane highway, there was almost no traffic except the occasional truck that roared past her or loomed in front of her, a dim shape in the falling snow. On either side, the plains stretched away into darkness.

She drove slowly. Usually it took about two hours to get from Boulder to her parents' home in the small town of Cottonwood Creek where she'd grown up. Tonight it would take at least three.

At last she came to her exit and could turn off the highway onto narrow, country roads.

She circled her shoulders and hitched herself to sit straighter in the seat. It had been more than two years since she'd been home; the sciatic pain had made it impossible to drive that far. But the road was familiar, no lights except for those in the occasional small town she passed through, then darkness again, her headlights barely piercing the falling snow.

No longer enough distraction to keep her thoughts at bay.

What am I doing? she asked herself. Running away? Abandoning my patients? Even through all the sciatic pain, the divorce, the moving, I never did that. I showed up, I hung in. But now ... She began to cry, tears stinging her eyes, her breath ragged. Her thoughts raced on. Now I don't know what to do. If I can heal everything with the Song, how can I turn anyone away? What right have I to ever rest? But if I don't rest, I can't go on forever. I'm only human.

At least with all those other difficulties, I understood the reasons for them. How can I ever understand what's happening now? Brenda says angels explain everything. But I can't believe in angels.

She wept harder.

Song rose in her, the gentle, comforting Song. Her weeping subsided to a few gasps. *Ah*, the sweet, unearthly voices sang. She held her breath listening. The Song lifted, floated, touched her with a soothing caress, then faded. Could anything but angels sing like that? Even though there were still tears on her cheeks, Harriet felt calmed.

It was all blessing, Brenda had told her, and she knew that was true. Blessing to be out of pain. As she drove through the snowy night, she marveled that, even though she'd been on the road for hours, there was not the slightest twinge in her leg. Blessing, too, for all her patients who were also out of pain, who had been healed by the Song. She thought of Janet with scoliosis whom she had been treating for more than a year with only slight results. What a gift it had been to at last be able to straighten and lengthen the spine, reshape the malformed ribs, create space and order for the organs.

The problem was that they all thought it was she who had healed them. Since she had kept the Song silent except for Jack, she couldn't explain that it was the Song. Couldn't explain anyway. Who would believe her?

If only she could talk to Neal, her mentor, her beloved. He would be there in Cottonwood Creek. For a few minutes, she let herself imagine running up the walk to the little yellow house that was his office, being folded in his embrace, sitting with him, sharing it all, knowing he would listen and understand as he always had.

But that possibility had ended decades ago. The old wave of grief washed through her. She pressed her lips together, pressing down the ache.

Ahead of her, across the dark plains, Harriet saw the lights of the next town. She glanced down at her gas gauge. Probably enough to make it, but better to be sure. Fortunately the town's only gas station was still open. Harriet got out, stretched, pumped her gas. As she got back into the car, she noticed the clock on her dashboard. Already 7:10. She'd told her mother she'd be there by seven, and she was still a half hour away.

She pulled out her cell phone and called.

"Hello." Her mother's voice quavered. Harriet visualized her in her old flowered apron standing in front of the phone on the kitchen wall, the only phone in the house.

"Hi, Mom. It's Harriet. I just wanted to let you know I'm running late."

"Oh, honey, I'm so glad to hear from you. I've been worried. I've made you a potpie, the kind you like. We're so looking forward to seeing you. Are you all right? It's snowing like the dickens here."

"It's snowing here, too, but I'm doing fine. Just driving slowly. I should be there in about half an hour. You and Dad go ahead and eat. But save me some of that potpie. I'll see you soon."

"Okay, honey. Drive careful."

"I will. Bye."

Harriet flipped her phone shut, tucked it under the dashboard, and started driving again. Mom sounds so old, she thought.

She hadn't seen her parents for two years, though they had talked on the phone almost every week. Her father would only say hello, then hand the phone to her mother. Her mother would talk, tell her news of the town and of the people she knew who were still there. She'd told Harriet that her father had gout and heart problems, but when asked about herself, would only say, "I'm fine. I get around."

Harriet wondered how she really was. I can help her now, she thought, with a rush of joy. And Dad, too, if he'll let me.

Her thoughts drifted back to the last five days. Only five days. So much had happened it felt like years. Remembering Morna Morningstar, Harriet started laughing. Then laughter spilled over into sobs. How could she, a decorous, professional chiropractor, have attracted someone like Morna Morningstar? Her whole world was topsy-turvy. Because she had grown up believing herself to be ugly and awkward, she'd never liked to be noticed by any but those closest to her. Now she was in the spotlight. And now she had received a gift she was running away from and could never be worthy of.

Why me? she asked herself. Why would they choose me? They? *Who are they?*

Her headlights shone only a short way into the tunnel of snow and darkness before her.

As Harriet approached her hometown, the first lights she saw were those of the bar, close to the side of the road, cars clustered around it. A little farther along, the gas station. Closed. Harriet was glad she had stopped for gas earlier. At last, after another half mile of darkness, she came to the town.

She sighed and relaxed her shoulders.

Cottonwood Creek was shrouded in snow, the streetlights shining through the drifting flakes. She turned down the quiet road that led to her parents' home. The porch light was on and the curtain in the front room drawn back.

As she hurried up the porch steps, the door swung open. "Here you are, at last!" her mother exclaimed as she pulled Harriet inside. Harriet dropped her bags and embraced her mother. She felt small and frail in Harriet's arms.

Inside it was warm and bright, a fire in the wood stove and the aroma of potpie drifting into the living room from the kitchen. Her father was settled in his big chair close to the stove, his swollen foot elevated. He turned his head and actually smiled at her.

"Hi, Harrie," he said. "Long time, no see."

She went to him and kissed his cheek. "I'm here now." He smelled of sweat and tobacco and the gin and tonic he was holding in his hand.

"We're so glad," her mother said. "We've missed you. We see Sophie most days, and Emma gets down to visit now and then, but it's been so long since we've seen you. Sit down now, honey, and talk to your dad. I'll bring your potpie in here."

Her mother always called her "honey." So did Brenda. Harriet liked that homey way of being told she was loved.

She followed her mother into the kitchen. "I'm not quite ready to sit yet. I've been sitting in that car for three hours. Let me help you."

"All right, honey." Her mother opened the oven and pulled out the potpie. "You can drive now? Is your leg really better?"

"It is. I'm so grateful."

"What happened? Did that last surgery work after all?"

"No …" Harriet didn't know what to say. She knew her mother wouldn't be able to handle a story of miraculous Song. While she thought how to answer, she reached into a familiar drawer and pulled out a hot pad for the potpie.

Finally she said, "There's something doctors call 'spontaneous remission' when they don't know why someone suddenly gets well. I think I had one of those."

"Well, I'm glad. I sure hated to think of you in all that pain. Come on into the living room and be comfy. I'm making some chamomile tea. Would you like some?"

"I'd love it." Chamomile tea had always been her mother's way of comforting her and soothing her childhood storms.

Harriet looked around the familiar kitchen and into the bright, warm living room. It was the same, exactly the same, as when she'd been a child, except that now her parents were old and her sisters were gone. As she carried her potpie into the living room and sat on the couch facing her father, she felt her body relax. It was as if she'd turned back pages in the book of her life and come to rest in a simpler time.

"How are you doing, Dad?"

Her father had always been gruff and taciturn. It had taken him years to forgive her for her youthful rebellion, but tonight he seemed genuinely glad to see her.

"Well as can be expected for an old man," he said. "My foot hurts."

"I'm sorry. Maybe after I finish eating, I can massage it a little for you."

"Touching it makes it worse."

Harriet winced inwardly at the all-too-familiar rejection. Never mind, she told herself. You know nothing you can ever do will please him.

Her mother came in with teacups on a tray and set it on the coffee table. "Here's your tea. I put in lots of honey the way you like." She sat down on the couch beside Harriet and handed her a teacup.

The potpie was delicious, the chamomile tea sweet.

"How are things going at the shoe store?" Harriet asked her father.

"Good, good. Jimmy's helping out, doing a good job. I have a family business after all."

He couldn't resist that jab about the family business, Harriet thought, but let it go. "I'm glad he's there to help you," she said.

She knew that his grandson Jimmy had started working there as a teenager, stayed on, and now in his late thirties had taken over managing the store. Her father went every day anyway, but mostly just sat around gossiping with whomever came in.

While Harriet ate, her mother talked, filling her in on the latest news of her sisters, Sophie and Emma, and their children. And the big news. There was a new minister in their church now, Reverend Winston Harvey, a widower, very handsome, a good preacher.

When Harriet finished eating, she moved closer to her mother and put her arm around her. She realized she was holding her breath. What would she see in her mother? Then the Song rose in her, and without even looking she could feel the fragility of her mother's bones, the unsteadiness of her heart, the tumor growing in her lungs.

Fear choked her. An involuntary gasp escaped her, and the Song died away. She hadn't had that happen before—the Song leaving before the healing was complete. But she had never been afraid as she was now. Her mother was infinitely precious to her.

Her mother turned to her. "Are you okay, honey?"

Slowly she drew in her breath, slowly let it out again. "I'm fine. It was just a half sneeze."

Help me, she prayed to the angels or whomever "they" were. A tender Song came into her, soothing her. The fear slipped away, and the healing Song returned. It was a struggle to keep it silent. Before she got it under control, a low hum escaped her. Then she settled into the now familiar trance, "their" love and hers flowing into the frail body in the curve of her arm.

Her mother sighed and laid her head on Harriet's shoulder. "You were always such a comfort to me," she said softly.

The fire crackled in the stove. Her father dozed in his chair, his hand curled around the empty glass resting on his belly. The Song rose into ineffable power and sweetness, strengthening the brittle bones, steadying the heart, dissolving the tumor. Her mother sighed again and slept, her head growing heavy on Harriet's shoulder. Harriet held her a long time after the Song faded away.

Chapter 7

Cottonwood Creek

Harriet woke the next morning in the bedroom that had been hers the last three years of her childhood. Before that, she'd shared the adjoining room with Emma. Only when Sophie went off to school had there been space for Harriet to have a room of her own.

She stretched under the comforter listening to the sound of the furnace rumbling. Hanging over the side of her bed, she opened the heat vent on the floor and felt the warm air flow up against her face. There had been many years when they'd had no central heating in the house, and the three girls would run downstairs on a cold morning like today to dress by the old, rattling gas heater in the living room. When Harriet was twelve, her parents had replaced it with the wood stove and installed a furnace in the crawl space under the house. She still felt it was a luxury to be able to open the vent and have the room grow warm while she was cozy in bed.

She lay on her back, her arms folded under her head, and thought of her sisters. Sophie was the golden child with her wide blue eyes and fair curly hair, her father's favorite, the prettiest girl in high school. She had always been blessed. Even though she'd gotten pregnant and had to get married, her husband, the son of a wealthy rancher, adored her and gave her every luxury possible. Over the years they'd raised three bright, handsome children in the big rambling house on the ranch. They had grandchildren now.

Sophie had been a hard act to follow. Harriet, born four years after her, didn't even try.

Their father was delighted with Sophie, his beautiful little daughter, but bitterly disappointed Harriet wasn't a boy. Even though she looked like him. Not such a blessing. Then a year later, Emma came along, the baby of the family, almost as pretty as Sophie. Growing up, Harriet had been well aware of the talk around town, that it was a shame Harrie was so plain, while her sisters were so pretty.

Both sisters had just the kind of lives they'd grown up to expect—good marriages, healthy children. But for Harriet, the plain one, the odd, quiet one, nothing had turned out as expected. Here she was at fifty-four, divorced, childless, blessed or burdened, she didn't know which, with a strange gift she had no idea how to handle.

The Song healed her mother, she thought, and felt a rush of energy as she remembered it moving though her as she held her mother in the curve of her arm. Her mother would have died soon with that tumor. Now she should live awhile longer.

Her father didn't look good. He may not let me touch him, Harriet thought, but I'll try.

She could hear her parents talking and moving around downstairs in the kitchen. Time to get up. What will I do now? she asked herself. I just ran—to a place I could hide for a while. But I'll have to go back. Maybe the uproar will die down eventually and I can just do my work as I used to.

She rolled out of bed and reached for her clothes, knowing such a wish was futile.

❧ ❧

"Be careful," her father said. "It hurts."

"I won't rub it," Harriet assured him. "Just let me hold it. I'll send some light into it."

"Hippie nonsense," her father said. "You've been living up in Boulder too long." But he let her take off the shabby slipper and wrap her hands around his swollen foot.

She almost jumped, jolted by what she saw and the power of the Song rushing into her. An odd sound escaped her before she gathered it into silence. The swollen foot was the least of his problems. She saw the arteries of his heart dangerously narrowed, the damage to liver and lungs, the high level of tension throughout his body.

The Song pressed against her hands. A wisp of it slipped into his foot, easing the swelling slightly, but no more could get through. It was as if he had armor around himself and the Song bounced off it. The rebound hit her in the solar plexus. After a moment the Song died away, leaving Harriet shaken by what she had seen, the intensity of the Song that sought to heal it, and the shock of rejection.

She sat a moment more, holding his foot, her head bent, seeking to recover herself.

Her father drew his foot away and laughed briefly. "I don't feel anything," he said. "Thanks anyway, Harrie. I've got to get along to work now. Saturdays are busy at the store."

She did notice that his limp was less pronounced as he shuffled out of the room.

Still struggling with the shock of the Song rebounding, she went to the kitchen to help her mother with the breakfast dishes.

"How's Dad doing?" she asked, as they moved into their familiar rhythm, her mother washing, Harriet rinsing and stacking. "I'm concerned he's still drinking. It's not good for the gout."

"Oh, you'll never get him to stop that," her mother said. "I do the best I can for him, but he's stubborn. You know."

Harriet did know. She watched her mother with tender concern. She knew her dad had only become more grumpy and difficult as he aged. It must be hard for her, Harriet thought. But her mother was strong in her own quiet way. She chattered as they worked, telling Harriet more about the new minister, how his sermons were much more inspiring than those of the old minister, who had recently retired.

Harriet looked out the kitchen window. The snow had stopped, and the sun was shining on a clean, white world. Jimmy had come by earlier and shoveled the walk and driveway before going to open the store.

"I'd like to take a walk," she said to her mother as she wiped down the counters, "see the town. Can I do anything for you while I'm out?"

"Oh, would you take back my library books? They're not due till Monday, but I'm finished with them. I'll get them for you."

Harriet loaded the books into her backpack and kissed her mother goodbye. As she stepped out the door, she took a long breath of cold, crisp air, the scent of snow. Peace flowed into her. All of her formative years, she had been nurtured by the quiet spaciousness of the vast plains stretching out to the horizon, the wide, high sky above. Main Street was the only street in Cottonwood Creek that went anywhere. All the other streets, including her parents', dead ended into grasslands or dwindled to dirt roads that wound away to the ranches scattered out around the town. Nothing interrupted the open expanse of the plains, not even a tree, except along the creek that flowed on the east side of town.

There were trees in town, of course, along all the streets—elms, cottonwoods, spruce, and locust, old trees planted when the town was new. They were bare now except for the evergreens laden with last night's snow.

Harriet started down the street. The neighbors, out clearing their walks, greeted her. "Hey, Harrie, where you been so long?" "Harrie, good to see you."

She stopped and chatted with each of the neighbors who greeted her, exchanging news of her family, their families, their other neighbors, the weather, the latest town happenings. It took her half an hour to walk the two blocks to Main Street. She'd forgotten what it was like to have everyone she met know her. Very different than walking down the street in Boulder.

Downtown Cottonwood Creek had hardly changed in the forty years since she'd been a child. The bank, the post office, the town hall surrounded by a lawn with the library in back, the tiny office of the town newspaper on one side of the street. On the other side of the street, the general store, the drugstore, her father's shoe store with the big sign, HARRY'S SHOES, over the door. The bowling alley was closed, boarded over. But Della's soda fountain, where they'd all gone to hang out after school, was still open, though Della, Harriet surmised, had probably passed on by now. Rick's Restaurant was doing a lively business that morning. On the corner of Grove and Main, the feed store was open, several trucks parked outside.

Harriet followed the walk around the town hall to the library. A new, young librarian sat at the desk. Mrs. Baker, who had been the librarian when Harriet was in high school and was still there the last time Harriet had come home, must have retired. Harriet missed her.

She swung her backpack down and took out her mother's books. Romance novels. *Why am I not surprised?* Harriet thought. *I can't imagine Dad giving her much romance.*

She returned her mother's books and had just reached the bottom of the library steps on her way out, when a male voice called, "Harrie!" Neal's son, Roger, strode across the lawn to her. He was tall, lean, and broad-shouldered like his father, and walked with the same easy grace. He held out his hand.

Harriet took it, smiling. She'd always liked Roger Walker. "Hi. How are you?"

"Fine. Good to see you. It's been a long time. What brings you home?"

"Just taking a break. Came down to see my folks."

"Your practice going well up in Boulder?"

"Full and overflowing."

"I'm not surprised. Dad always said you'd be really good."

Harriet caught her breath, swept with memories. Neal. His blue eyes bright and attentive as he listened to her questions. His hands guiding hers to palpate, on her body or his, the spine of a vertebra, the head of a femur, the shape of the sacrum. All his support for her dream of becoming a chiropractor. The grief of their estrangement surged up.

Harriet jerked herself back to the moment, to Roger. "How's your family?"

"Fine. We've got three kids now. Little Mark arrived last summer."

"Congratulations. And your parents?"

Roger turned his head away briefly, biting his lower lip, then looked back at her. "You didn't know?"

Harriet's heart tightened. "No. What?"

"Mom died. Last October. All of a sudden. A heart attack."

Harriet's own heart started beating fast. Sarah dead! Then— "I'm so sorry," she managed to say. She hesitated, swallowing a lump in her throat. "And your dad?"

"Not good. He's got cancer. Diagnosed last summer. He stayed around long enough to welcome little Mark into the world, then went off to some fancy cancer center in California. You know him, everything alternative—support groups, diet, cleanses. He didn't even consider radiation and chemo. When he came back for Mom's funeral, he looked awful. I'm afraid we're going to lose him, too. I get real mad at him, but he won't change his mind. Says he's had a good life, maybe it's time, and all. It's his choice."

Harriet felt a chill spreading through her, stopping her breath. She found she was pressing her fingers against her lips.

Roger watched her, concern growing in his face. "I'm sorry to give you the bad news," he said. "I remember you worked for him when you were in high school, running his office."

Harriet moved her hand away from her mouth and pressed it against her heart, which was now racing out of control. She struggled to keep her voice normal. "He was real good to me. Encouraged me. Helped me get a scholarship to the university."

"That's how he was." Roger sighed. "I've got to get going. Good to see you, Harrie. Drop by and meet the new baby." He turned to wave as he walked back across the lawn.

Momentarily frozen, Harriet stood at the bottom of the steps, her hand still pressed against her heart.

Then she ran.

Chapter 8

Love and Rebellion

At the edge of town, a dirt road wound along beside the creek. It was hardly a road, just a rutted track.

Harriet had little awareness of how she'd reached it. She vaguely remembered running down Main Street, turning off, and dashing past the few houses at the edge of town. At first she had just run, reeling from Roger's news, but once she left the plowed streets, she stumbled in ankle-deep snow and slowed to a walk.

The sun was winter low in the sky even at midmorning, slanting through the cottonwoods and Russian olives that hung over the creek. She came to a place where the creek bank sloped off steeply with a cluster of tamarisks at the top. Above them she could see the tips of two tall rocks. Without intending to, she had fled to her secret childhood hideout. As she pushed through tamarisks that had grown thicker over the years, snow fell on her in soft clumps, brushing her face with a cold caress. She climbed up and turned sideways to slip through the space between the two rocks, then dropped down into her niche. A hidden place where no one could see her, a refuge she had sought not only in childhood but often when she came back to visit. Below her the creek was a mottled pattern of snow and open water, its voice a low gurgle in the silence of the morning.

She pulled the hood of her down jacket up over her head, brushed snow aside, and curled into the hollow at the base of the two tall rocks. Wrapping her arms around her legs, she bent her brow to her knees.

Sarah dead. Neal sick, maybe dying. Far away in California. Even though she had not spoken with him for more than thirty years, just knowing he was in Cottonwood Creek had anchored her.

Now she felt cut loose, adrift. It was impossible to imagine him dying. He had always been so strong, so vital.

She had known him all her life. The town was so small everyone knew everyone and everyone's family and everyone's business, even the name of the family dog. Neal was a chiropractor, the only one in that part of the county, the only doctor of any kind in Cottonwood Creek. His children, Roger and Nan, were six and eight years younger than Harriet. His wife, Sarah, hosted a quilting circle that Harriet's mother participated in.

But it wasn't until an afternoon in April the year she was sixteen that she noticed him. He was Dr. Walker to her then.

Harriet was working in her father's shoe store. The bell over the door rang and Neal came in.

"Hi, Dr. Walker," she greeted him. "Can I help you?"

"Hi, Harrie. Sure. I need some new tennis shoes." He stood on one leg, perfectly balanced, bent the other leg up with his knee turned out, and tapped the worn-out sole of his shoe. "Like these, if you have them."

"I think we do."

"How are you?" He had a kind smile.

"Fine." Harriet bent her head, hiding her face behind the long fall of her hair. She led him past racks of boots to a shelf on the back wall. "All our tennis shoes are here."

Her father came over—and took over. "Neal," he said in his booming customer voice. "Good to see you. What can I do for you today?"

"Harrie, here, was helping me. I'm looking for another pair of tennis shoes like these, if you have them."

"Sure we do. What size?"

"Eleven and a half."

"Harrie." Her father turned to her. "Get Dr. Walker some size eleven and a half tennis shoes. You want blue again?" he asked Neal. "We've got black and orange, too."

"Blue will be fine."

As Harriet retreated to the stock room, she heard Neal ask, "What's wrong with your girl?"

"Nothing. She's fine."

"She's limping. It looks like she's in pain."

"Oh, that." Harriet could hear her father settle into his gossip voice. "She got the crazy idea she wants to be educated, go to college and all. I told her I wasn't paying for it. It's a waste of time to educate a girl. I sent Sophie to secretary school. She dropped out after six months and got married. Never worked a day. But Harrie's a stubborn one, already putting on airs, talking like her English teacher. So off she went and got a job mucking at Joe's horse place. Got kicked by a horse. I told her she'd be safer working here."

Harriet *hated* it when her father talked about her that way. Even in the privacy of the stock room, she felt herself blushing.

"You ought to bring her around to my place and let me straighten her out," she heard him say.

"Can't afford that. She'll get over it."

"I think she needs some attention," Neal insisted. "Tell you what. Stella's getting old, talking about retiring. I'll be looking for some part-time help in my office. If Harrie wants to come work for me after school, I could give her some of her pay in adjustments."

In the back room, Harriet stood still, listening. Someone noticed, someone cared that she limped, that she hurt. Her dad sure didn't. Hot tears stung her eyes.

"She's working for me now," her father said. "Harrie," he called. "When you bringing out those shoes?"

Just then the bell over the door rang again, and her father bustled off to greet the next customer.

Harriet rubbed her tears away with the back of her hand and reached for the box of size eleven and a half blue tennis shoes. She pulled in her breath, held it a moment, then stepped out of the back room. Bending her head so the fall of her hair shielded her blushing face, she took the shoes to Neal, opened the box, and folded back the tissue paper.

"Is this what you want, sir?"

"They look perfect."

"Would you like to try them on to be sure they're comfortable?"

"That sounds like a good idea." Neal sat down and pulled off his old shoes. One of the things Harriet hated most about working for her father was how bad his customers' feet smelled. Like old sweat and manure. But Neal's feet didn't smell at all. His socks were clean, gray with blue toes and heels.

Kneeling in front of him, Harriet took out the new tennis shoes and looked up at him. His eyes were blue, too, with laugh wrinkles at the corners. She liked the way his big hands lay open and easy on his knees. He was smiling at her.

Gripping the shoe in her hands more tightly, she stammered, "I heard what you said to my dad … Thank you for offering to help my back … for noticing. It does hurt … a lot." She hesitated, still looking up at him, then said in a burst, "I'd like to work for you."

"I'd like to have you." He touched her shoulder. "And I think we can get you straightened out and feeling a lot more comfortable."

His touch was gentle, his eyes kind, his voice deep and resonant.

She fumbled with the shoe. "I'd work hard. I'm careful. I'd do a good job." Then overwhelmed by her boldness, she bent her head again, hiding her face behind her hair.

Neal leaned over and took the shoe from her, brushing her hand with his. Harriet could feel the blush rising in her cheeks.

"I'm sure you would," Neal said. "I've heard you do real well in school. But what about your job here?" He slipped his foot into the left tennis shoe and laced it up.

"I don't like working for my dad," she blurted. She looked up at him again. Her mind raced. "Henry Taylor, he's in my class, was telling me he wanted a job. He could have this one."

Neal flexed his toes and ankle in the new shoe.

"I know Henry. He's a responsible boy. That would be a good solution. So, if it's okay with your dad, come by tomorrow after school. I'll have Mrs. Sanders show you the ropes and we'll do some work on your back."

"I'll come." She smiled then, hope bursting inside her.

"You have a beautiful smile," he said, smiling back at her.

No one had ever said such a thing to her, the plain one. In that moment, Harriet fell in love.

That evening as she and her parents and her younger sister Emma were sitting around the table after dinner, she told her father. "I'm quitting at the shoe store. I'm going over tomorrow to start work for Dr. Walker."

"Wait just a minute." Her father drew his brows together, the frown line between them deepening. "You can't just quit. I'm counting on you."

"Henry Taylor wants a job. I already told him I'm quitting. He can take my place. He's coming over tomorrow to talk to you."

"No." Her father pushed back his chair and towered over her. "Henry's not family. My shoe store is a family business. Your mother does the bookkeeping and you—I need you. I'm counting on you to take over the store when I retire."

Harriet stood up, too, and faced her father. She was as tall as he and met him eye to eye. "You never asked me about that."

"Crimminy," Emma muttered, and scooted out of the room. Harriet could hear her running up the stairs. Her mother made an incoherent sound and fluttered her hands.

"I thought you understood that when I hired you," her father said.

"I certainly didn't." Harriet felt blood rush to her face. "I hate working in your store. All those ranchers' stinking feet. And you never pay me. I've been working for you a month and not a cent. You said you'd put it in my bank account every week. I checked it today and you haven't put any in. Joe paid me every Friday."

Her mother was shaking her head from side to side. She reached out a tentative hand toward Harriet. "Honey . ."

"What do you need money for?" Her father's voice was dangerous. "I give you a good home, feed you. And you'll inherit the store."

"So you never intended to pay me?" The red rage Harriet felt rising in her frightened her, but she couldn't stop. "You were planning to keep me working for you without pay except that I would inherit the store in the far future? You lied to me. You said you would pay me." She drew in a deep breath. "Get this. I don't *want* to inherit the store. I need money because I want—to go—to college." She was speaking between clenched teeth. "And you won't help me. So I need a job where I'll get *paid*."

Her father drew his chest up; his frown deepened. "You're wasting your time. There's no use educating a girl. Look at Sophie."

The sting of being compared to Sophie for the umpteenth time pushed Harriet over the edge. "I'm not Sophie. No one's going to marry me. I wasn't so lucky as to look like Mom the way Sophie and Emma do. I have the misfortune of looking like you, bony and ugly with that big nose of yours stuck in the middle of my face."

"Enough!" her father bellowed. He stepped up to her and slapped her hard across her face. "Don't ever talk to me that way again."

The room reverberated with shocked silence. Harriet put her hand on her burning cheek.

Her mother half rose from her chair and reached out to her. "Harrie—" she began.

Harriet whirled and faced her. "Don't call me Harrie, ever again. I'm not a boy. I'm a *girl*. From now on call me Harri*et*. I don't like that name either, but at least it's a girl's name. Why didn't you give me a pretty name like Sophie and Emma?"

Her mother sank back into her chair. "Your father wanted to name you after him."

Harriet's hand was still pressed against her cheek. "Right. Another Harry Ellis to run the shoe store. You wouldn't even have to change the sign." She spun to face her father again. "You laid that on me from the moment I was a newborn baby, and this is the first I hear of it? Well, forget it. I'm never setting foot in that shoe store again. I'm going to work for Dr. Walker starting tomorrow. He'll pay me. And he'll help my back. He cares that I'm hurting."

She struggled with the grief that was threatening to choke her. "You don't even care. 'She's fine,' you tell Dr. Walker. 'I can't afford to fix her.' Just so you know, I'm *not* fine." Sobbing, she ran out of the room.

Later her mother came upstairs and sat beside her where she lay face down on her bed. She'd stopped crying, but her fists were still clenched under her chest.

Her mother smoothed her back. "I'm sorry your back is hurting. I didn't know it was so bad. You don't complain like Emma does." She stroked Harriet's head. "Don't mind your father. He was just so disappointed you weren't a boy. I thought he'd get over it, but he's stubborn. Had his heart set on a son to carry on the business. He was so pleased when you came to work for him."

"He could have paid me. It's not my fault I'm a girl."

"Of course it isn't."

"Even though I don't look like one, flat chested and ugly and taller than any boy in my class."

"Honey, you're not ugly. You have really pretty hair. And a sweet singing voice. I was so proud of you when you sang the solo in church last Sunday. And your teachers say you're smart and you work hard. You're a good girl."

Harriet rolled over on her side. "Please don't call me Harrie anymore. I hate it. It's so confusing. I don't know whether you are talking to me or Dad."

"I'll try to remember."

She didn't remember, of course. No one did, even when she started asking people to call her Harriet. She'd been Harrie too long. The whole town knew her by that name.

Neal was the only one who remembered. The very first day she worked for him she asked him to call her Harriet, and he never forgot.

❧ ❧

Harriet snuggled deeper into her jacket. Even with the sun out it was cold, and cold spread up into her from the rock she was sitting on.

"Come back," she whispered to herself, fighting the grief that washed through her in waves. "Come back to now."

But now—now Sarah was dead and Harriet had the Song. Neal was sick, but maybe she could fly out to California and sing for him, and the Song would make him well. They could finally be together.

She lifted her head, her jaw tight. What are you thinking of? she asked herself fiercely. Why would he want me now? I'm no longer a young, sweet teenager. I'm fifty-four with wrinkles around my eyes and mouth, my hair graying and cropped short.

And besides, he told Roger it was his time. Would it be wrong to use the Song to heal someone whose time had come?

Oh, I don't know. I don't know.

Chapter 9

Invitation

Sophie, her daughter Mary, and Mary's three little ones were there when Harriet got back from her walk.

Sophie came to hug her before she even took off her coat. "Mom said you were here. I couldn't wait to see you. It's been so long. How are you?" She stepped back and looked up into Harriet's face.

Harriet returned her hug. "I'm fine," she said. She laid her cheek against Sophie's hair and held her close, warmed by Sophie's loving embrace. Although Sophie had paid little attention to her younger sisters growing up, a warm friendship had developed between Harriet and Sophie after they were grown. Harriet had often visited Sophie out on the ranch when she returned to Cottonwood Creek, and had cuddled Sophie's babies and played with her children as they grew.

Mary, with her baby on her hip, came to hug her next. She was the youngest of Sophie's three and had always been Harriet's favorite. Her two little boys clung to her pant legs. Harriet squatted down to greet them.

Her mother had lunch all ready; soon they were all settled around the kitchen table.

Still dazed by the news about Neal, Harriet felt as if she were in a time warp as she looked around the table. Although she was as pretty as ever, Sophie had aged. Her waist and bosom were fuller, there were lines around her eyes and mouth, and some white blending into her blond curls. The last time Harriet had been home, Mary had had only one child, a little boy a year old, and now there was another little boy and a baby girl. How could so much have changed when the house and the town seemed unchanged?

The baby was sick with a runny nose and a deep cough, flushed with fever. "She got this nasty cold from the boys," Mary explained as she rocked her baby in her lap. "They're fine now, but she's having a hard time."

Harriet's mother served up a beef-vegetable soup and hot biscuits. Sophie asked Harriet again how she was, was her back better? What about the divorce? Harriet's mother wanted to know why she'd been gone so long on her walk. But conversation was difficult. The two little boys needed constant attention, and the baby grew more and more fussy. Finally she began crying, which aggravated her cough. Sophie had her hands full supervising the little boys, and Mary began to look somewhat desperate as she jiggled the baby on her knee and tried to eat.

"Jenny, hush," she said.

Harriet pushed back her chair and held out her arms. "Let me take her," she said. "Maybe I can soothe her."

Mary looked doubtful. "I don't think she'll let you."

"Let me try. I'll sing to her."

"That might work," Harriet's mother said. "Harrie has such a pretty voice."

"Sure, anything." Mary handed the baby to Harriet.

At first Jenny stiffened and resisted Harriet's embrace, but when Harriet began a low hum, she softened.

Cradling the child in her arms, Harriet went into the living room. Back and forth she walked, singing soft and low. Even though she muted it, the Song poured through her with all its beauty and power. After a few turns around the living room, Jenny stopped crying and laid her head on Harriet's shoulder.

Harriet moved her hand over Jenny's back, found the congestion in her chest and felt the Song disperse it, moved her hand up to cup Jenny's head and felt the Song clear the sinuses and bring down the fever. Jenny took a long, deep breath and fell asleep. Still singing, Harriet sat down on the couch, gathered the sleeping baby closer, and laid her cheek against Jenny's soft hair.

After a while, she became aware that it was quiet in the kitchen. No one was talking, and even the shrill voices of the little boys were silent. Mary tiptoed into the living room. The Song faded away.

"Is she sleeping?"

Harriet nodded.

"Thanks, Aunt Harrie. You have a magic touch. That was a beautiful song you were singing. Even the boys quieted down. Shall I take her? Grandma has a crib upstairs in Aunt Emma's old room. She'll probably nap now, and you can finish your lunch."

Harriet stood, reluctant to let go of the child's sweet warmth nestled against her bosom. Moving slowly so as not to wake the baby, Harriet handed her to Mary.

Back in the kitchen, the little boys looked up at her with round, solemn eyes. Sophie and her mother gazed at her wonderingly.

"You always had a real pretty voice," her mother said, "but I never heard you sing so beautiful as that … What language were you singing?"

Harriet blushed. "I didn't know you could hear me … No language, just a baby song." She sat down, bent her head, and picked up her soup spoon.

Mary came downstairs and into the kitchen. "She's zonked," she said, "sound asleep. The first time she's slept like that since she got sick. Her fever's gone, and she's breathing easy."

Harriet's mother got up. "Let me get you some fresh soup," she said, taking Harriet's bowl. "And you, too, Mary. Your soup's gotten cold while you were tending the baby."

Mary stood by the table looking at Harriet. "What did you do, Aunt Harrie? She was really sick, and now she seems fine."

"I only rocked her and sang to her," Harriet said. "Her fever was probably due to break."

"But all her congestion is gone, too. She's not coughing and rasping like she was."

Harriet was struggling to think of something to say when she was rescued by her mother bustling to the table with two fresh bowls of soup.

"Sit down now, Mary," her mother said. "Here. Both of you eat your soup while it's hot." She turned to the boys. "Harry, Timmy, are you finished? Let's get your blocks out."

She and Sophie settled the boys in the corner of the kitchen with a box of blocks.

Harriet had almost forgotten that Mary's older son was named Harry. This place is lousy with Harrys, she thought. Grateful for the distraction of boys and blocks, she ate. She was hungry after her long walk, and her mother's soup and biscuits were delicious.

Sophie came back to the table and sat facing Harriet. "How are you doing really?" she asked. "Mom said you've had a hard time with the pain in your leg and the surgeries. You seem to be walking okay now."

"I am. The pain is all gone."

"I'm so glad. But you've gotten divorced, and you had to move out of your beautiful house. We've been so worried about you. Everything hard coming at once. What happened with you and Jared? Last time you were down to visit, you guys seemed fine."

"We were never fine. He's pretty self-centered. When I was tied down with pain and surgeries, he got bored with me. So he started going out by himself and found a younger woman. As some men do in midlife."

She folded her lips together and was silent, holding back a rush of grief and anger. Her mother touched her hand. Sophie and Mary gazed at her with compassion.

"It's better it's over," Harriet said. "I'm fine, really. It's a huge relief that the pain is gone from my leg. My practice is full. And I have a nice condo, with a little backyard and patio and space to grow a garden in the spring."

She smiled then, feeling another rush of emotion. Gratitude. She really *was* fine. So grateful for her healing, and for the Song and the love and the ecstasy of feeling it move through her. Grateful for her family, her mother's love, her sister and niece and the little ones.

Mary had finished her soup and was staring at Harriet. "What did you do, Aunt Harrie?" she asked again. "That song was so beautiful. I never heard anything like it before. And you were shining—"

The doorbell rang.

"Now who can that be?" Harriet's mother asked. She got up from the table and hurried through the living room to the front door.

"Reverend Harvey!" they heard her exclaim. "What a pleasure to see you. Come in. Come in."

"That's the new minister," Sophie told Harriet. "I wonder why he's coming by."

"Mom told me you had a new minister," Harriet said, glad to change the subject.

At that moment the little boys got into a fight. Harry hit Timmy over the head with a block and Timmy started screaming. Mary jumped up to intervene.

Harriet's mother called, "Harrie, come meet Reverend Harvey."

As Harriet came into the living room, her mother was talking fast, her face all lit up. "This is our Harrie," she said. "She's the one I was telling you about, that we've been so worried about, who had such a bad time with those back surgeries and got a divorce and lost her home and—"

"Mom." Harriet held up her hand. "Please."

Reverend Harvey was not quite as tall as Harriet. His gray hair was swept back from his brow, and he had kindly, blue-gray eyes under thick eyebrows. "I heard you were in town," he said, holding out his hand to Harriet. "I've come by to meet you."

"Word gets around fast," Sophie said laughing, as she came into the room with a tear-stained Timmy on her hip. "We're so happy Harrie's come to visit."

"Let me take your coat," Harriet's mother said, fluttering her hands. "Would you like some tea?"

"Thank you, Mrs. Ellis." Harriet liked the respectful way he spoke to her mother as he handed her his coat. "Some tea sounds nice." He turned to Sophie. "Sophie, it's good to see you. Is this your grandson?"

Sophie beamed with pride. "This is Timmy."

There was another howl from the kitchen. Mary came in leading a weeping Harry by the hand. "Mom," she said to Sophie, "the kids are overdone."

"Yes," Sophie agreed. "We should go and let Reverend Harvey have a quiet visit with Harrie."

Reverend Harvey and Harriet stood by as Sophie and Mary bundled up the little boys in their parkas and boots. Sophie took them out to the car while Mary went upstairs for Jenny. She stopped in the living room on the way back with the sleeping baby in her arms. "I can't believe the fever's gone and she's sleeping so peacefully. Really, Aunt Harrie, what did you do? Was it your beautiful singing that made her well?"

"I'm so glad she's better," Harriet said. She put her arm around Mary's shoulders and gave her a squeeze, bent and lightly kissed Jenny's brow. "It's good to see you again, and your little ones." She shivered inside. How did people guess about the Song? First Leah, now Mary.

Sophie stuck her head in the front door. "The boys are all buckled up. Are you ready?"

The living room was quiet after they left. Harriet turned to Reverend Harvey. "Won't you sit down?"

"Thank you."

He chose a rocking chair, and Harriet settled opposite him on the couch. Her mother came in with a tea tray. "You came to meet our Harrie?"

"Yes." He smiled at Harriet. "When I heard that you'd come home to visit, I also heard that you sing beautifully. Which your niece just confirmed. Several people have suggested that I ask you to give us a solo in the service tomorrow. As you used to do. They thought it would be a nice way to welcome you back. Would you like to do that?"

Harriet felt a quiver of fear in the pit of her stomach. "It's been a long time—"

"That would be lovely," her mother interrupted. "She was just singing here a little while ago to soothe Mary's baby, and it was so pretty even the boys quieted down to listen. You'd love to, wouldn't you, Harrie?"

"Well …" Harriet hesitated.

"We'd appreciate it," Reverend Harvey said. "Folks enjoy a new face, a new voice, and you are kindly remembered here, from what I've heard."

"I didn't think anyone would remember me," Harriet said. "I moved away years ago."

"But you come back to visit," Harriet's mother said. "Lots of people remember you, and we're all so proud of you becoming a doctor."

Reverend Harvey was watching her face. "What do you think, Harrie? It wouldn't have to be anything fancy, just a hymn that you like."

"Please call me Harriet."

"That's right." Harriet's mother waved her hands. "She asked us to call her Harriet. So we don't mix her up with her dad. But it's so hard to remember."

Reverend Harvey met Harriet's eyes with a twinkle of understanding. "I'll remember," he said.

Harriet softened. "What is the theme of your sermon for tomorrow?" she asked.

"I'll be talking about surrendering to God's guidance."

"Do you know the hymn, 'Lead Kindly Light'?"

"I do. That's a fine one. I haven't thought of it for a while. It would go perfectly with my Scripture from Psalm 25. 'Make me to know thy ways, O Lord, teach me thy paths.' Will you sing it for us then?"

"Oh … okay."

"Fine. Why don't you come by a half hour or so before the service and run through it with our organist."

He set down his teacup and stretched his legs. "I need to move on. I have a few more calls to make this afternoon." He stood and held out his hand to Harriet. "It's been a pleasure meeting you, Harriet. I'll look forward to hearing you sing tomorrow."

Harriet sat on the bed in her upstairs bedroom, her clenched hands pressed against her cheeks. *What have I gotten myself into?* she asked herself. *What if I can't control my voice and the Song comes out? The congregation's bound to be full of people with ailments. What if as soon as I look at them—?* She imagined gossip buzzing around town that she'd stood up to sing in church and let out all these strange words and weird noises. She'd always been considered a little odd. That would cap it. Her parents would die of embarrassment. What if the whole congregation freaked out and started running out the doors?

The fear that had quivered in her belly when Reverend Harvey asked her to sing morphed into full-blown panic. *I have to call Reverend Harvey,* she thought, *and tell him I can't. I've gotten an attack of laryngitis. Something.*

Softly at first, then more fully, singing began within her, the same soothing song that had come to her after she healed Tiger and last night when she became so afraid for her mother.

She could almost hear words. Not with her ears; the voices sang inside her. *Do not be afraid,* she seemed to hear. *We are with you.*

"That's just what I'm afraid of," she burst out, speaking aloud in the empty room to the presence she felt within her. "The Song sounds so strange. They will think I've gone nuts. I just want to sing the hymn."

The presence grew even stronger. She sensed bewilderment, questioning. *Hymn?*

"Just let me sing the way I used to," she said.

The presence seemed to listen.

Harriet took a deep breath, straightened her back, relaxed her hands in her lap and began to sing.

> "Lead kindly Light
>
> Amid the encircling gloom,
>
> Lead thou me on …"

Her voice was richer and fuller than it had been before the Song came to her, but there were no harmonies or overtones, and the words were English.

Maybe it would be okay.

Chapter 10

Are There Angels?

*M*orning light slanted through the tall windows of the church. The service was underway. Harriet liked the unostentatious way Reverend Harvey was leading it. The minister before him had had a special voice he put on to preach and read the Scripture. It had always annoyed Harriet; it was so clearly fake. Reverend Harvey spoke in the same grave, quiet voice he had used to converse with her the day before.

Harriet sat up front with the choir and looked out over the congregation. Her parents were there in their usual place. Sophie and her husband, Jimmy, and his family, Mary and her husband sat in the pew behind them. Filling the other pews were people from all the walks of life in that small town: wealthy landowners, teachers and shopkeepers, laborers, old and young. A wave of love for them all washed over her.

Her throat tightened as she realized it was the same quality of love that was the essence of the Song. *Would* she be able to just sing the hymn or would the Song pour out of her in all its strangeness? She didn't have to look hard to see there was need enough in the congregation to evoke it.

Reverend Harvey was reading Psalm 25. The Scripture. Her solo was next. For a moment she had the desperate impulse to run. But it was too late.

Reverend Harvey closed the Bible, turned and nodded to her. The organist played the opening bars. Harriet stood, her arms hanging in the folds of her choir robe. She didn't need music. She'd known this hymn by heart for years. With a brief prayer to the presences of the Song, she drew in her breath and sang.

"Lead kindly Light
Amid the encircling gloom,
Lead thou me on …"

After the first few bars, her fear faded. She was singing the hymn, English words, and at the same time the Song was singing through the hymn, pouring its blessing on the congregation. The sweet, ecstatic trance came over her; the love swelled within her. Line by line, her voice grew richer and fuller until the entire congregation was enfolded with her in the trance and the love.

When the last chords of the hymn faded away, the sanctuary was hushed, resonating with the glory of the Song. After a long moment, the people began to stir in the pews, looking around as if just waking. Harriet sat down and bent her head feeling as if she, too, were emerging from a dream.

When she lifted her eyes, Reverend Harvey was gazing at her, wonder on his face, a tear sliding down his cheek. "Thank you, Harriet," he said, his voice husky. Then he turned to the pulpit and began his sermon.

Harriet hardly heard him. She kept her head bent, her eyes down, not wanting to meet curious glances. It went all right, she told herself. *I didn't sing that strange language. I felt the Song, but I didn't see into anyone's body. I think I need to touch to do that. The love was there. I think everyone felt it. That's okay. It's in church, so they'll think it was God's love. Maybe it is.*

During the final hymn, Harriet sang softly, not wanting her voice to stand out from the others. Her head still bent, she filed out with the choir at the end of the service, but once in the choir room, she couldn't avoid the exclamations and questions from the choir members.

She knew most of them—neighbors and former teachers, childhood classmates, their grown children, their parents. They pressed around her.

"That was so beautiful." "I never heard you sing like that before." "Your voice was just heavenly."

Harriet felt the old instinct to slump and duck her head, but her hair wasn't long enough now to hide her face. And she had outgrown that, she reminded herself inwardly. She drew in her breath and held her head up. Still, the discomfort of being the center of attention became intense. As briefly as she courteously could, she responded to the compliments, then slipped out the back door into the parking lot.

The congregation was just coming out the front door. She ducked behind the parked cars, ran down a near-by alley and out onto the quiet street a block away. From there it was only a short walk to her parents' house.

Later that afternoon, as Harriet's father dozed in front of the TV and Harriet helped her mother wash up, the phone rang. Her mother answered it.

"Oh! Hello, Reverend Harvey." Her voice grew breathless. "Yes … wasn't it beautiful? … Yes, she's here. Just a minute." She turned, the receiver in her hand, her eyes wide. "Harrie, Reverend Harvey wants to speak with you."

Harriet dried her hands and took the phone. "Hello."

"Hello, Harriet. I'm calling to invite you to have tea with me at the manse this afternoon. I'd like to talk with you. Could you come?"

Harriet's heart started pounding. Had she done something wrong? But he *asked* her to sing. She remembered his face after her solo, the tear on his cheek. He might understand, she thought. Maybe he could help me. Do I dare confide in him?

"Harriet?" His voice questioning.

She realized she hadn't answered his invitation. "Yes. Yes, thank you. I can come. What time?"

"How about 3:30?"

"That would be okay."

"Fine, I'll see you then."

"Okay. Bye."

Harriet's mother fluttered her hands. "What did he want?"

Harriet was beginning to realize her mother had a crush on the new minister. She knew it was not uncommon for older women whose husbands paid little attention to them to fall in love with the minister, and Reverend Harvey—handsome, mature, eloquent—was a perfect object for such frustrated longing.

"He invited me to tea at the manse," Harriet answered. "He wants to talk with me about something."

Harriet's father shuffled into the kitchen and opened the refrigerator. "What's the preacher want to talk to Harrie about?" he asked. He took down a glass from the cupboard and mixed his drink.

"About her singing, I bet," her mother said. "It was so beautiful. Everyone was talking about it after the service. They were all looking for you, Harrie. Where were you?"

"I'm sorry. I just slipped out the back door. I figured you'd guess I'd be home."

Her mother touched her shoulder. "You shouldn't be so shy. You're fine. And so talented. We're very proud of you. Aren't we, Harry?"

Her father didn't answer. Drink in hand, he shuffled out to his chair in the living room.

Harriet felt her jaw tighten as she watched his broad back retreating.

"Don't mind him," her mother said. "He *is* proud of you. He just doesn't like to say it."

Harriet looked down at her mother, glad to see the pink in her cheeks that meant she was getting enough oxygen again. "Thanks, Mom," she said. She bent and kissed her mother's brow.

"Now," her mother said, "you should change your clothes. You can't go see the minister in jeans and a sweatshirt."

The manse was a modest house next door to the church, two blocks south of Main Street. The walkway was neatly shoveled and there was still a wreath on the door, even though the holidays were over.

Harriet paused on the porch. During the walk over she had resolved to confide in Reverend Harvey. He seemed like the kind of minister who would keep confidences. And maybe … She really didn't know what she wanted to ask him.

She rang the bell.

"Come in." He greeted her with a welcoming smile. He was wearing a blue plaid shirt open at the neck and gray slacks. "May I take your coat?"

She hesitated, feeling overdressed. Jared had always insisted on her being clothed in the latest fashion and had taken her shopping—often over her protests—to expensive shops to outfit her for the next important event in his professional and social life. Today she wore a green velvet sheath dress, one of her favorites of his choices. She'd been startled to see, looking in the mirror as she dressed, how it enhanced the color of her changed eyes.

Reverend Harvey hung up her coat and ushered her into the living room. "Please sit down. I have black tea or herb tea. Which would you prefer?"

Harriet smiled. "Herb tea sounds good. You're going to revolutionize this town. I didn't think anyone in Cottonwood Creek, except my mom, ever heard of herb tea."

Reverend Harvey chuckled. "Peppermint?"

"Perfect."

Once they were settled with their tea, Reverend Harvey said, "I wanted to ask you about your hymn this morning. Something extraordinary happened when you sang."

Harriet put her hand to her throat and swallowed. No words came out.

He watched her, kindly, waiting. "Were you aware of that?" he asked finally.

"Yes."

"Can you tell me about it?"

Still she struggled for words. Finally, to her surprise, she blurted out, "Do you think there are angels?"

"Angels?" He sat back, his eyes wide in surprise. "I don't know quite how to answer that. Certainly there are many references in Scripture. And certainly there are many instances of humans acting like angels, ministering to each other." He paused. "But perhaps I could answer you better if you'd tell me why that question is important to you. Because I see that it is."

Harriet realized that her hand had moved from her throat to press against her heart. "It's important," she said, "because … something happened to me, just a week ago, that changed my life … and the only thing that could possibly explain it … is angels. But I don't think I believe in angels. And anyway, why would they care about me?"

"If there are angels," he said, "they are ministers of God, and God cares about everyone. Would you be willing to tell me what happened to you?" Feeling her hesitation, he added gently, "Everything between us is confidential."

"Okay," She drew in her breath. "I was taking a walk at night a week ago Friday." She would *not* tell him about the suicide attempt. "I took a short cut across the lake. The ice broke and I fell in. It was in the middle of the night. There was no one around. I should have died."

He was leaning forward in his chair now. "What happened then?"

"I don't know. I don't remember anything until Sunday morning. I have no idea how I got out of the lake. Just a week ago, though it feels like it's been forever."

She plunged on, telling him about singing on the hillside, the heavenly voices singing with her, the unbroken snow, the Song coming when she held Tiger, little Jack, and all the events of the last week.

"Then I ran away." She stopped speaking, biting her lower lip, afraid she'd said too much.

Reverend Harvey had been listening intently, the expression on his face shifting in response to her story, a look of growing wonder in his eyes. "Because it was overwhelming?" he asked.

"Yes."

"I can understand that. But Harriet, this is amazing. Such a blessing you have been given. Do you have any idea, any clue …?" He broke off, shaking his head.

"I haven't told you about the dreams, the voices inside me."

"Please tell me."

She told him about the words that came to her occasionally, the iridescent bubbles, the love, the soothing song that came when she was frightened, her frustration at not remembering what they taught her in her dreams. "But I feel as if I'm beginning to be able to communicate with them a little," she said, realizing as she spoke that it was true.

Reverend Harvey rubbed his chin, shifted in his chair. "Maybe I'm all out of line to ask this," he said. "But I would really like to hear the Song, the way you sang it for little Jack, out loud. Would you sing it for me?"

"It doesn't come unless there is need, unless I touch."

"I'm having a problem with my back. I wrenched it shoveling snow yesterday morning. I wouldn't mind if you touched me."

Harriet smiled. "I'm used to touching, you know. I'm a chiropractor."

"That's right. Of course."

There was an awkward silence.

"Okay." Harriet said. She stood up and went behind the chair where he was sitting.

She laid her hands on his shoulders, and her vision opened. It wasn't a severe injury, just a twisting of the lower spine, which often happens with snow shoveling. Something she could easily handle with a chiropractic adjustment. But there was also arthritis in his hips and knees, not severe but could become so.

The Song welled up in her. It was such a relief to not have to hold it in silence. Glory, power, and love poured through her voice. Wrapped in the trance, she sang; and when the Song died away, the spine was straight, and new cartilage filled the joints that had been worn down.

Harriet lifted her hands from his shoulders and went back to her chair, shaken as she always was coming out of the Song, but even more so now, feeling that she had revealed herself to someone she barely knew.

He sat quietly opposite her, tears running down his face. Then he sighed, wiped his cheeks, stood, and walked around the room. "It's all better," he said, touching his back. "But I knew it would be the minute you started singing." He stopped in front of her. "To tell you the truth, I don't know much about angels. Ministers don't know everything. But— that was heavenly music. It could only have come from God."

"Please don't tell anyone. It gets complicated. That's why I ran away. But already here …"

"Yes," he said. "Your niece was quite interested in how quickly her baby got better. You sang for her?"

"I had to. She was so sick. It might have gone into pneumonia."

He touched his back again. "It really is all better. Thank you, Harriet."

"It wasn't me. It was the Song."

"'Not I, but Christ in me,'" he quoted softly. "St. Paul." He sat down again across from her. "What an amazing gift. What an amazing day! What will you do now?"

"I don't know. I think I have to go back."

"I think you do, too."

"But it's overwhelming. I wish I could understand what they are saying to me."

"I think it is important that you continue to try to communicate with them. Maybe they could teach you how to manage the Song, how and when to use it."

"Maybe. It seemed yesterday—I got so frightened. I was going to call you and tell you I had laryngitis. But then they sang their comforting song and seemed to understand when I told them I just wanted to sing the hymn. And it came out okay this morning. The Song didn't come. Only the love came."

"Surely," he said, "the love is God's love. I felt it. Everyone did. It filled the church. And your voice was like the singing of angels. Do you think it was those beings that appear to you as bubbles that pulled you out of the lake?"

"They couldn't be. They're not real. Just dream images."

"Yet they try to communicate with you, teach you." He shook his head, a quizzical expression on his face. "It's a wondrous mystery. Miracles do happen, Harriet. And it seems you have been the recipient of one."

"But I'm just an ordinary, middle-aged woman," Harriet protested. "I'm not especially good or anything. Actually, I'm kind of awkward. And I don't know what to do. It got crazy back in Boulder with people just coming into my office without appointments, begging me to sing and heal them. I can't say no. I know what it is like to have pain; I want them to be better."

"Perhaps the hymn you chose to sing this morning can help you. 'Lead kindly light.' Especially the last line 'One step enough for me.' I suggest you go back and pray each day, each moment if you need to, for guidance. Surely God, having given you this gift, will show you how to use it."

"I'm not particularly good at praying. I know there must be a God, but I'm not very well acquainted with Him."

"Then pray to the angels, the bubbles, if that works better. Surely they are part of God. We all are."

"That's rather radical theology," Harriet said, beginning to smile. "Maybe you really are going to revolutionize this stuffy little town."

He shrugged and grinned. "Maybe. Don't tell."

They laughed together.

Harriet felt her heart lighten, realizing she probably could learn to communicate with the bubbles, the angels. That she already had. And that they loved her with a quality of love that must be like God's love.

"Okay," she said. "I'll pray to the angels."

Chapter 11

The Little Yellow House

"How long can you stay?" Harriet's mother asked at breakfast the next morning.

"I think I need to go back tomorrow."

"That's a pretty short visit," her father said, looking at her over his coffee mug.

"It seems like you just got here," her mother said.

"I can come again before too long. Now that I can drive again. But I need to get back. I have a lot of patients needing my attention."

"We've hardly seen you," her father said.

Harriet was astonished and touched that her father seemed to mind that she'd be leaving. "I'll be here today."

"I'll be in the store."

Harriet reached over and touched his hand. "I'll stop by and see you."

"I thought you said you'd never set foot in my store again."

"Dad, that was almost forty years ago. I've been there lots of times since then. I'll come by today. Maybe we can catch a visit between customers."

It was all pretense, Harriet thought. Jimmy and his two clerks handled the store efficiently. Her father wasn't needed at all, but it was important to him to think he was.

After she helped her mother clean up the breakfast dishes, Harriet went up to her room and called Brenda.

"Hi, there, honey," Brenda greeted her. "I was wondering when I'd hear from you. How's it going down there in the boonies?"

"Livelier than I'd hoped, but I've gotten some clarity. So I'm heading back tomorrow. How are things there?"

"Well, it's a crazy Monday morning. I'm at the office now. Thought I'd catch up a bit while you were gone. Your voice mail's full and the phone's been ringing off the hook. Good you called my cell or you would never have gotten through."

"What have you been telling people?"

"I haven't. I don't know what to tell them, so I haven't answered."

"I'll drive back tomorrow and can start seeing people on Wednesday."

"Okay, I'll start scheduling. But just so you know, I'm not putting in more than your usual twelve a day and none on the weekends. Someone's got to look after you."

"Thanks, Brenda. What would I do without you?"

"You don't have to. How are you doing? Did you get any rest? You didn't go healing everyone there, did you?"

"A few. My mother. But I did rest. I'm doing all right. I'll give you a call when I get in tomorrow."

"Okay, honey. Drive careful."

Harriet sat a moment with the phone still in her hand. I'm really going back, she thought with a shiver of apprehension. Oh, my God, what will I do?

She got up, pulled on her jacket and went downstairs. "I'm going for a walk," she called to her mother, as she went out the door.

❧ ❧

She stood in front of a small, ranch-style house on a quiet street two blocks from the creek. The yellow paint was faded and peeling. The blinds were drawn, the walk unshoveled, the front steps and porch piled with snow.

Even though she'd visited Cottonwood Creek often since she moved away, she hadn't walked on that street for thirty-one years. Not since the day Neal sent her away. She hadn't dared the risk of being seen there, of seeing him or having him see her.

There was no danger now. He was far away. A knot tightened in her belly. The little house looked so neglected.

Time folded. She saw herself, a tall, awkward sixteen-year-old, approaching the house for her first day of work for Dr. Walker. It was April. There were golden daffodils and blue forget-me-nots blooming in the narrow gardens on either side of the walk. The yellow paint was bright and fresh, the front door open to the balmy afternoon.

Her heart was pounding, all her instincts telling her her life would change when she stepped through that door.

As it had.

Mrs. Sanders greeted her warmly. "Here you are, Harrie."

"Hi," Harriet answered. She hesitated in the doorway, looking around.

The living room had been divided by a waist-high counter into waiting room and office. Mrs. Sanders sat behind the counter at a wide desk with a typewriter, a telephone, and piles of papers and notebooks. File cabinets lined the wall beside her and a bookshelf filled with fat volumes stood against the back wall. In the waiting room were a beige couch with dark green pillows, two upholstered chairs in a lighter green, and a coffee table with magazines and a pink potted geranium. On the wall facing the couch was a large photograph of a mountain scene with white peaks, tall evergreens, and a rushing stream. A hallway led off the waiting room.

Mrs. Sanders eased her plump, elderly body out from behind the desk. "I'm glad you're here," she said. "I've been needing some help. Let me show you around."

She led Harriet through a door in the back of the office that opened into a kitchen. "This is our private place, for staff only. You can put your book bag here on this shelf. Here's a place to hang your jacket. If you need a snack, there's some cookies here. We've got milk in the fridge for coffee, but there's plenty if you'd like a glass. Dr. Walker's with a patient now. The bathroom's just down the hall. Get yourself settled and then we'll start."

The phone rang, and Mrs. Sanders went to answer it. Harriet set down her books and hung up her jacket, then tiptoed down the hall to the bathroom. On either side of it was a room with a closed door. Harriet could hear Neal's voice and the voice of a woman coming from one of the rooms. Her heart beat faster.

For the next two hours she sat beside Mrs. Sanders at the big desk, learning how to keep the books. It wasn't hard for her; she had a good mind for detail and privately thought she could do a neater job than Mrs. Sanders. She listened carefully to how Mrs. Sanders answered the phone.

"Hello. Dr. Walker's office. This is Stella." Mrs. Sanders chatted with whomever she spoke to. Harriet didn't think she would do that; she'd just stick to business. And she was determined to say, "This is Harriet" not "Harrie." Maybe a few people would get the message.

Patients came and went. Many were people Harriet didn't know as they came from surrounding towns. Neal came out to greet each one, then took his patient back to the treatment room. Whenever he appeared, Harriet's heart flip-flopped. The first time he came out, he greeted her. After that, he looked over and smiled at her. She loved his smile and the way it crinkled the corners of his eyes. When his back was turned, walking down the hall to the treatment room, she gazed at him, adoring his lean grace.

The last patient left a little after five. Neal sat down on the edge of the counter. "How's it going?" he asked.

"She's doing fine," Mrs. Sanders answered. "A quick learner like you said she'd be. I've got her going on keeping the books. Tomorrow I'll start her answering the phone."

"Great," Neal said. "I'm going to give her a treatment now. You can go home. Come on back, Harrie."

He led her to one of the rooms at the end of the hall. "Undress down to your underwear and put on this gown with the opening in the back."

He left and closed the door. Harriet bit her lower lip. She didn't have a bra. She'd never worn one because her breasts were so small. She hadn't shaved her legs. He was going to see her body. He was going to touch her.

She took off her clothes and fumbled with the gown. How could she tie it in back? She could manage the top tie, but couldn't reach the others without twisting, and twisting hurt a lot.

He knocked on the door and she came out, hiding her face behind her hair. Her gown was still open in the back and she knew he could see her plain cotton underpants.

"I couldn't tie it all the way up," she explained, blushing. "It hurts to twist."

"It's okay," he said. "I'd just untie it anyway." He led her to the room across the hall and gestured to a narrow table with a white sheet on it. "Come lie here, face down. Let's see what we can do about that horse kick."

Harriet felt his hands on her back, on her skin. An unfamiliar heat swept through her. She gasped and hid her face.

"It's okay," he said. "I won't hurt you."

Step by step his strong, gentle hands guided her body out of its twist. When she stood at the end of the session, she exclaimed in astonishment, "It does feel better."

"I would hope so," he said, smiling at her.

"How ... how did you do that?"

"It's my craft. Chiropractic."

As she walked home that afternoon, feeling the new ease in her body, all her yearning to go to college, to learn, to do something that mattered came into focus. She would become a chiropractor like Dr. Walker and help people who were in pain.

From that moment on her life had meaning. Each afternoon after school she went to Neal's office. Mrs. Sanders taught her how to schedule appointments, order supplies, bill insurance, pay the estimated tax, keep the books—everything that was needed to manage the practice.

Sometimes when a client came out, Dr. Walker handed her a slip of paper telling her to charge an amount less than his usual fee. Sometimes the note even said "no charge," and Harriet quickly understood that he knew some of his patients would have difficulty paying in full. He's so kind, she thought, loving him even more. He cares more about his patients than making lots of money. She couldn't imagine her dad charging less than full price for any of his shoes, even if the customer were poor.

When school let out for the summer, Mrs. Sanders retired and Harriet worked full time. By that time she had learned to handle everything efficiently, and Neal was very pleased with her performance. He paid her every week, and her little bank account grew.

Three times a week, after the last patient, he took her into his treatment room and worked with her body. She looked forward to those sessions in a confusion of eagerness and trepidation. Before long she recognized her sensations as sexual. After all, she'd seen movies, witnessed her classmates kissing and groping behind the school steps. She comforted her shame by telling herself it was because she loved him so much. At night she lay awake lost in fantasies of kissing him and holding him in her arms until she burned with passion, and touching the most afflicted place, found herself wet.

As the weeks passed, she dared to imagine that he returned her attraction. He often stroked her bare back as she lay face down on the table at the end of the session. When he moved her long hair aside to work with her upper back, he'd pause to run his fingers through it.

"Your hair is beautiful," he said once. "So shining and soft. Like silk."

But, of course, he was married.

Often as they looked at the day's schedule together, he'd put his arm around her shoulders. Once, when she leaned her head against him, she felt him tighten and pull away, and she cringed with shame. At times, she'd look up from her desk to find him gazing at her with such tenderness that she felt her heart would melt. But whenever she met his eyes, he'd look away.

He began giving her a hug before she left for the day, holding her close for a long moment.

One morning, when they were going over the day's appointments together, he said, "You don't need to call me Dr. Walker. Call me Neal. You're my partner now."

Harriet's heart swelled with happiness. She knew she was doing a good job and was proud of it. Having him call her his partner blew her fantasies wide open. She turned to smile at him with all her love shining in her eyes. This time he did not turn away, but met her gaze, his blue eyes soft with tenderness.

"Okay, Neal," she said.

No one in Harriet's life had ever been as kind and attentive to her as Neal was. During a break in his schedule, he'd come perch on the edge of the counter that separated her little office from the waiting room and ask her about her life. She soon found herself pouring out her dreams and struggles. Often he had just the piece of wise advice that helped her face a social embarrassment or deal with a fight with her father. As she shared her dream of becoming a chiropractor, he encouraged her to get good grades so she could get a scholarship. She was already a good student, but became determined to get all As when she went back to school for her junior year.

Once the effects of the horse kick were eased out, Neal continued to work on straightening Harriet's upper spine, which had fallen into a curve from her habit of ducking her head and slouching to hide her height. Neal encouraged her to stand straight and hold up her head. It felt scary at first, but it also felt better.

"You look elegant when you stand that way," he told her.

So she tried to remember and began to feel more confident and graceful. Best of all, she was rewarded by his approving smile.

As the summer moved on, Neal began not only to listen to her, but to share with her. They had long talks at the end of the day. Harriet learned about Neal's boyhood in the mountain town of Evergreen, west of Denver. She learned that he had come to chiropractic as she had, to be healed from an injury, a ski injury in his case; that, even though he loved the mountains, he had come to Cottonwood Creek out on the plains because there was need there, no doctor closer than the town of Elizabeth, thirty miles away. His wife, Sarah, had reluctantly come with him and then had become the social center of Cottonwood Creek. In bits and pieces, a few words at a time, Harriet learned that Neal was unhappy in his marriage, though he was devoted to his two children. His wife was too busy with her social rounds to pay much attention to him. There were even hints they rarely had sex.

Hearing that, Harriet vowed fiercely that if she were his wife, she would love him every day, welcome him any time he wanted. She sometimes fantasized that Sarah would divorce him or die. Then she would be ashamed and address herself intensely to her office work.

In her first chiropractic sessions, Harriet had simply surrendered to Neal's touch, washed in all the sexual and sensual sensations that arose. But toward the end of the summer, she became curious and started asking Neal what he was doing and why. So he began to teach her.

She was thrilled, fascinated. She started hurrying through her work to have time to study the big anatomy books and chiropractic texts on the shelf in the office. At first they were hard to understand; it was a whole new language. Neal answered her eager questions and referred her to the medical dictionary, and soon she began to grasp what she studied. Sensual anatomy lessons became part of the erotic tension between them, as he touched on her body the places she asked about. She wasn't sure if he was just teaching her, or if he wanted to touch her as much as she wanted him to.

When school started in the fall, she feared he would hire someone else, but he said, "No, look at this. An answering machine. It will take calls when I'm working, so I can take care of the basics by myself in the morning. Then when you come in the afternoon, you can return calls and handle everything as you do so well. I'll need you to work a half day on Saturday to catch up on bookkeeping. Can you do that?"

Of course she could.

So the next two years passed. Harriet's connection with Neal transformed her from a lost, awkward child to a young woman, still shy and introverted, but with clarity and focus. She did get all As when she went back for her junior year. During her senior year, Neal helped her prepare for college entrance exams, research the best schools to attend, and apply for scholarships.

The relationship between Harriet and Neal continued to deepen. Harriet became increasingly sure that Neal returned her love and that he struggled with it as she did. So she was no longer hurt when she saw his jaw tighten and felt him suddenly pull away from what threatened to become a too-intimate moment.

Then came the end of Harriet's senior year. She was valedictorian of her class and had won a full scholarship to the University of Colorado in Boulder. When school was out, she worked full time for Neal, as she had the proceeding two summers.

They were together all day again. Hands brushed, eyes met, touches lingered. Harriet's loins ached for him, her arms yearned to hold him, she felt her heart would break apart with love for him. And with each touch, each meeting of eyes, she felt the urgency of his desire matching hers. The eros between them stretched to the breaking point.

It was Harriet who crossed the line. One afternoon, at the end of the work day, as Neal held her close in a long hug, she softly kissed his cheek and whispered, "I love you." Neither one had ever spoken those words to the other.

He tightened his arms around her. "I love you, too. So much." He lifted her chin and kissed her mouth. She returned his kiss with all her pent-up longing.

Later, they lay naked side by side on the treatment table. The white sheet was stained with Harriet's virgin blood and Neal's semen. He had withdrawn at the last minute.

Harriet tentatively stroked his side, marveling in the feel of his skin, the muscles beneath it, the wonder of their skin touching. Her head rested on his shoulder. He ran his fingers through her long, loose hair. She felt she could die from the sweetness of his touch.

He let out a sound, half sigh, half moan. "Harriet, my sweetheart, I shouldn't have. I lost my head. Forgive me." He started to move away from her.

She clutched at him. "No. Don't. Don't go away. I've wanted you from the first time you touched me. I love you more than anyone in the whole world."

"And I," he said, stroking her hair, "have never known such love as I feel for you." He turned her face to look into her eyes. "I've been holding back ever since you smiled at me the day you sold me shoes in your father's store."

"*Really?* That's when I fell in love with you."

"Ah, sweetheart." He gathered her close again, kissing her cheek, her neck, her lips. "It started then and just grows deeper the more I know you."

"It's the same for me," Harriet whispered.

Neal shifted a little, cradled her cheek in his hand. "But Harriet, we shouldn't let this happen again. There's no future for you in getting involved with a married man."

"But I *am* involved." Harriet tightened her arms around him. "I'll never love anyone but you."

"You're too young."

"I'm not too young. My mother was my age when she married my dad."

He groaned. "What can I do? How can I resist you?"

They kissed again, caressed, made love again, lay limp in each other's arms, washed in bliss.

After a long while, Neal said, "No one must know. We could get into a lot of trouble."

"I understand. I can keep a secret."

And, over all the years, she had.

Harriet was cold. She shuddered and brought herself back to the quiet street, the empty house in front of her.

How long have I been standing here? she asked herself. Good grief, if anyone sees me, they'll think I've gone nuts. She glanced around, but fortunately no one was in sight.

The day had turned cloudy and a sharp wind had come up. Harriet tightened the strings of her hood under her chin and started walking. Before long she was striding down the dirt road by the creek. More memories flooded over her.

Once the barriers were down they made love almost every afternoon after the last patient had left. Harriet would always remember those times. Summer sounds coming through the curtained windows: the clickity clack of a lawn mower, bird song, the occasional passing car, sometimes the thunder of an afternoon storm. The smell of rain, new-cut grass, the tang of his sweat, the taste of his mouth, his weight over her, the pungent odor of his semen. Above all, the wonder of being loved, held, desired.

As summer moved on she became afraid she would get pregnant as Sophie had. Only Neal wouldn't be able to marry her. At first she didn't care. Nothing mattered but his touch, his love. But at last the worry became great enough for her to speak.

"I mustn't get pregnant," she said.

"No, indeed," he answered. "Don't worry. I'm taking care of that." He showed her the condom he was wearing. She'd never noticed it in the passion of their foreplay. After that she relaxed, trusting him.

That summer was the happiest time of Harriet's life. Being with Neal all day and at last being able to give her love full expression was more joy than she had ever thought possible. He was her lover, her mentor, her confidant, her best friend, the center of her life.

Then it was time to go to college. Leaving him was like tearing her heart out. She clung to him, weeping as she kissed him goodbye.

He held her close. "You'll be back," he said, "and we'll love again."

She took his words into her heart and, fired by their promise, earned her Bachelor of Science in three years by taking extra courses each semester and during the summer. She kept to herself, known by other students as the odd one, the grind.

On holidays she came back to Cottonwood Creek, ostensibly to visit her family, but her heart was focused on Neal, burning for him, longing for him. He would meet her at his office at the end of the day—she told her parents he was tutoring her—and they would seize each other and fill the treatment room with their passion.

She graduated with honors and her parents, even her father, came to her graduation. Neal did not. "We must be careful of rumors," he told her.

Then for three long years she did not return to Cottonwood Creek. The Palmer College of Chiropractic was in Davenport, Iowa. It was too expensive to make the trip back to Colorado. Anyway, she studied through every break, working her hardest. She longed to be in touch with Neal but didn't write to him, fearful that her letter might be intercepted by Sarah or his new office manager; but she thought of him always, holding her dream in her heart. After she earned her Doctor of Chiropractic, she would return to Cottonwood Creek, become Neal's partner, and never leave him.

The day she returned from Iowa, she ran to his office in the late afternoon after she knew the last patient would have left, to tell him she was home to stay, that she could be with him again, be his partner in the practice.

He met her in the waiting room. Gently, he withdrew from her embrace and held her away from him, his hands on her shoulders, his eyes both sad and hard. "No, Harriet," he said. "We can't."

"Can't?" Harriet's belly contracted. "What do you mean, we can't?"

"This is a small town. You're not a kid anymore. You're a full-grown woman, and quite attractive."

"We could be very careful. No one ever knew before."

"There were rumors that only died down when you were gone. If you came back now and joined the practice … We can't."

Harriet was so stunned she couldn't speak. As her dreams shattered, she felt her blood rush from her face, tears spring to her eyes. Her hand went to her throat.

Neal's expression softened. "Come sit down." He guided her to the old beige couch and pulled up a chair opposite her. "I'm sorry. I didn't realize you were planning this. I thought you'd know it was impossible. Please understand. I have a wife who would be very upset if she knew about us. I have children in high school. You know how vicious the gossip can get in this town."

"But …" Harriet's words came out in gasps. "It was all I wanted, all these years … ever since you started teaching me … to be your partner, help you like I used to." She pressed her hand against her mouth, struggling with her tears.

"Harriet, think of your life. I know how you love children. I've heard you speak many times of Sophie's little ones. You'll want to get married and have a family of your own. I can't marry you. You need to let go of me so you can move on."

Tears were running down Harriet's cheeks. She shook her head from side to side. "I'll never love anyone but you."

"Of course you will. You have a deeply loving heart, and your life is just beginning."

Harriet squeezed her eyes shut and bent her head so hard she pushed her chin into her throat. Her breath stopped. Realization, like a huge, dark wave, crashed down on her, pounding her onto rocks of shame. She'd made it all up. All those years she'd studied her hardest and built her dream, she'd made it up. He'd never promised she could come back and work with him, be his partner. He'd never invited her. Of course it was impossible.

She covered her face with her hands.

When at last she could speak, she lifted her head. "What will I do now?"

"You will be a chiropractor," he said gently, "An excellent one, and help many people with your skillful hands."

"But … where?"

"I have thought about that. I knew you would be home soon and was hoping to see you. I have a plan I would like to share with you. I have a colleague in Denver, Eliza Reilly. She and I were classmates. She's wanting to slow down a little and would like someone to share the load. I've told her about you and she said she'd be happy to have you join her practice."

"Denver?" Harriet felt a cold stone drop in her belly.

"I know it's a big city, but you'll find your way around, and once you get some experience, you can move to a smaller town. Eliza's a good practitioner. She'll help you get started."

Harriet couldn't hear him anymore. Doubling over, she buried her face in her lap and sobbed. She felt his hand on her shoulder. His dear hand, his beloved touch.

"Sweetheart, I'm so sorry. I never wanted to hurt you, but now I have."

Harriet drew in her breath, biting her lip. Fumbling in her pocket, she found her handkerchief and blew her nose. "Okay," she said. "I understand. I'll go." Her tears started again. She held out her hands to him. "Love me, one last time."

Longing, then resolution crossed his face. "No. It would only make it harder."

He got up and went to his desk, came back with an envelope in his hand. "Here is information about Eliza Reilly and also the address of a woman who rents rooms in her house just a few blocks from Eliza's office."

He held out the envelope. She stood and took it. She swallowed. For a moment, everything went dark. Then she came back to see him standing in front of her, his face mirroring her desolation. "Go," he said.

She turned and fled.

That had been thirty-one years ago. Harriet hadn't seen him since, except for the few times they had passed on the street and she had turned her head away without answering his greeting.

It had been a dream of child-like innocence. Neal had done the only thing he could and, even in sending her away, had given her references for a position and a place to live.

How could it still hurt so much after so many years?

Chapter 12

The Song Bounces Back

The bubbles floated around her; haunting, unearthly harmonies poured through her.

Harriet woke from her dream and turned in her bed. Except for the faraway sound of a passing car, the night was silent. The Song was within her, permeating every cell, rich with meaning she couldn't quite grasp.

She sat up, the bedding in a tumble around her, her hands pressed against her chest.

Please, please, she prayed, *help me understand.*

She kept her eyes closed, her whole being taut like a tightly strung harp string waiting for a magic touch that would decipher the singing, bring her clarity.

But the voices drifted away, the bubbles faded to a mere shimmer and then were gone.

Harriet's awareness came back to the small bedroom of her condominium, the streetlight outside casting a yellow square on the wall opposite her, the smell of snow coming through the half-open window. She was cold. She jumped out of bed and dashed across the room to shut the window. Back in bed, she pulled the covers up around her chin and tried to relax, to recall the dream, to listen.

Something came. A single word—*eliria*. She spoke it aloud, "Eliria," and felt, as if in response, a vibration in the air around her, a tingling within her. "Eliria," she said again.

She waited. The tingling dissipated. Nothing more came. She switched on the light, saying the word over and over again. I mustn't forget it, she said to herself, as she threw back the covers and hurried into her study to write it down.

Pencil in hand, she asked herself, "Is it with an 'i' or an 'e'?" She wrote it both ways, studied it. Somehow the "e" felt better. She pulled her dictionary out of the bookcase and opened it on her desk. No *eliria* with an "i" or with an "e." Not an English word then.

Her mind reeled. Why would angels speak English?

If there are angels.

But it was a clue. She got up and paced the small room. "Eliria," she said the word aloud. "I wonder what it means. It's a lyrical sound. Like the singing."

She went to the window and looked out. Above the bare tree branches, cold winter stars pierced the night's darkness. "What does it mean?" she asked the stars.

The stars did not answer.

❧❧

The office was warm and bright with the morning sun shining in the south windows. Brenda hurried to embrace her.

"Here you are," she said. She stepped back to look up at Harriet's face. "You look a little tired. Did you get back late last night?"

"No, I got home mid-afternoon, time to go to the store and settle in. But I didn't sleep well. I guess I'm kind of anxious about today."

"It'll be all right, honey. I've got your patients lined up. You do have a full day, but I'll be guarding the door. Don't worry. You just do your thing and everyone will be blessed."

"Thanks, Brenda. Let me see this morning's folders."

The morning went smoothly, though at first it was an effort for Harriet to keep the Song silent. It felt so much better to sing it aloud as she had done for little Jenny and Reverend Harvey. But she soon moved into the trance of the Song, barely emerging between sessions as she said goodbye to one patient and greeted the next. Love poured through her, and the deep bliss of finally being able to completely heal her patients.

Her last patient of the morning was a man named Ron, whom she had seen occasionally over the last year. He was in his late sixties, a Vietnam vet who wore a brace on his leg. His leg had been shattered in a war injury and never healed properly, causing him to twist around his hip as he walked. This awkward gait caused him chronic back pain.

As she watched him limp in, Harriet felt a rush of joy. At last she would be able to mend the leg bones so he could walk normally again and be out of pain.

"Let's start with your leg," she said as he settled himself on the table.

"Never mind the leg. That's hopeless." He glared at her from under bushy gray eyebrows. "Just fix my back."

"Let me just check your leg. I have an idea."

"Don't waste time on it."

Ignoring his resistance, Harriet laid her hands on either side of his lower leg. The Song rose up in her and her vision opened just long enough for her to see how the shattered bones could be mended. Then the Song bounced back into her, jolting her.

Ron sat up and pulled his leg away. "What're you doing?" he growled. "I said, leave the leg alone. It's my back that hurts."

Anger flared in her, and the Song was gone. She palpated Ron's back, found the usual subluxation, and went to work in her old way, massaging the muscles on either side of the spine, then doing her well-honed chiropractic adjustment. It felt heavy and cumbersome after the gentle flow of healing with the Song.

At the end of the session, Ron limped out. Brenda looked up as he passed through the waiting room, raised one eyebrow, and shot a glance at Harriet.

Harriet ducked back into the treatment room and shut the door. She sat on the treatment table and pulled her knees up to her chest. Why does the Song bounce back? she asked herself. Why did it bounce back from Dad? Don't they want to be healed?

If only I could talk with Neal. He would help me understand. Struggling with the old longing, she bent her brow onto her knees.

"Hey, Harriet." Brenda knocked on the door. "Lunch time."

Once they were settled in the back room with their lunches, Brenda asked, "What happened with Ron? He looked as grumpy as ever when he left."

"The Song bounced back."

"What?"

"Yeah. It happened with my dad, too. He wouldn't let it in. I tried twice, once the first night I was there, and again on Monday. That time I tried to be real sneaky, visited him in his store and stood behind him with my hands on his shoulders. Keeping it all silent, of course. It still bounced back, but not before I saw how much he needed it. His heart and liver are in bad shape, and he still drinks. I'm afraid he won't last much longer."

"That's tough. And with Ron?"

"Same thing. I started to work with his leg and he jerked it away and told me to just fix his back. Then the Song went away. I did my usual thing, like I used to. Maybe it helped a little."

"Weird. Why do you think it bounced back?"

"I'm not sure." Harriet was thinking as she spoke. "Maybe the Song only works if the person wants to be healed. Maybe Ron's leg being injured is part of his identity, his hero stuff. If it was all fixed and he walked normally, then people wouldn't know. He wouldn't be special that way anymore."

"That makes sense."

"But even if they do want to be healed, what if it's God's will that a person—maybe their injury or sickness is part of their karma, their punishment. And I'm interfering. Maybe I shouldn't—how would I know?"

"Whoa, honey. Easy. You got this Song. Sounds like heavenly music to me, the one time I heard it when you sang to that boy Jack. Seems like it's a gift from God. So if God gave it to you, He's not gonna be mad at you for using it. Seems to me if their karma is to keep their pain, the Song bouncing back handles that. How does it feel when it bounces back?"

"Awful. Like I've been hit in the solar plexus. And the worst of it is, just before it bounces back, I see what's wrong, and then I'm really upset that I can't fix it."

Brenda reached across the table and patted Harriet's hand. "Eat your lunch. We don't need the Song bouncing back to tell us nobody can be fixed if they don't wanna be. We knew that. Some folks just love their suffering."

Harriet ate, realizing with the first bite how ravenous she was. For a while they ate in silence.

Then Harriet said, "I dreamed again last night. The bubbles, the singing. I still couldn't understand what they were trying to tell me, but when I woke I heard a word in my head. Eliria. I felt like it came out of the singing. I looked it up. There isn't any such word in the dictionary, but it felt like a clue."

"Eliria. It's a pretty sound. Those bubbles. Does it feel like they're people? I mean I know they're not people. I don't know how to say it."

"It feels like they have consciousness, intelligent, compassionate consciousness. I don't think the bubbles are their real shape, just how they appear to me. I keep saying 'they' as if there really are presences, beings. But maybe it's all a dream left over from the shock of almost dying. If there really is someone, something there—someones, because it does sound as if there are many—then they must be the source of the Song. And the healing."

"Do you think they were the ones who pulled you out of the lake?"

"The minister in Cottonwood Creek, Reverend Harvey, asked me that, too. But I don't think they're physical. So how could they?"

"The minister in Cottonwood Creek? Did you tell him about the bubbles?"

"I told him everything—except the suicide bit."

"How come?"

"I sang in church."

"No way! What happened then?"

Over the rest of the lunch, Harriet recounted her adventures in Cottonwood Creek. All except for the news about Neal and the memories that came as she stood in front of the abandoned house with the peeling yellow paint.

That evening, as she prepared to go home, Harriet looked through the window in the front door at a cluster of people waiting for her to come out.

"What will I do, Brenda?" she asked. "There are more than ten people out there, and the minute I step out, they'll all be begging me to heal them. I'll be working all night."

"You will not. Climb out the window in the back room. I'll go out and talk to them. We have a schedule. They need appointments."

"But what if someone is in crisis?"

"I don't know. I just know you can't work all night and still be good the next day. Now go on, out that back window. Maybe before you sleep tonight you should ask them, the bubbles, what to do about the crowd at the door. Maybe they'll give you an idea."

Feeling guilty, Harriet climbed out the back window. Her car was there in the small parking lot behind her office. It's only a matter of time, she thought as she drove home, before the back window is discovered. Then what?

That night before she slept, Harriet sat on the edge of her bed, and spoke the strange new word: *eliria.*

"Help me," she whispered. "There are so many who need the Song, and I am only one mortal woman. Tell me what to do. And please help me understand your voices."

Chapter 13

Messages

She woke the next morning knowing she had dreamed, knowing they had been with her, feeling they had given her something, but unable to remember what. She got up, pulled on her robe and went to her study. The winter morning was dark, and she could see through the window that it was snowing again. She sat down at her desk, turned on a light, and pulled out a pad and pencil.

Maybe if I listen, meditate, I will remember their message, she thought. She drew in her breath and spoke the strange word, "Eliria."

A shiver went through her. She quivered all over like a leaf in a sudden gust of wind.

Waited.

No Song came, but an idea. What if I leave one appointment a day open, maybe the last one, that would be available for emergencies? The rest could wait for regular appointments.

She shivered again. That's a good idea! That would help a lot. I wouldn't feel so bad if I had some space for accidents, like Jack's, or serious illnesses, like little Jenny's.

She wrote the idea down on her pad. Then waited again. A thread of Song wound through her. And there were words, heard inside her. Her hand trembled as she wrote:

Do not be afraid to sing aloud. It is better that way.

"Really?" she asked the silent room. She lifted her head to listen, her pencil poised over the pad. "It does feel better. It's hard to hold it silent."

Another thread of Song within her. Just one voice, bright, clear, bell-like.

It is not good to hold it back. Holding it back will block your … The Song hesitated.

"Block what?" Harriet asked.

But the Song was gone. Only another strange word remained: *tirini.* Harriet wrote it hastily. *Tirini.* What could that mean?

She jumped up and began pacing her small apartment, alive with excitement, her thoughts racing. *I got a message. Two messages. Keeping an appointment open each day for emergencies and singing aloud. And a new word. Tirini. I wonder what it means. Maybe they have their own language. But they seem to know mine. I can't wait to tell Brenda.*

⮌ ⮎

She went to the office early, hoping to have time to talk with Brenda before her first client arrived. There was already a small gathering outside the office door when she came around the corner of the building.

"Good morning," she greeted them as she tried to weave her way between them to the door. A large, obese man blocked her way.

"My name's Karl," he said, holding out his hand. "I've heard you are good with knees. Mine hurt so badly I can hardly walk. I'd like to see you today."

"I'm sorry. Today is full, but you can make an appointment with my assistant by calling this number." She pointed to the sign Brenda had put on the door.

"I can pay you double," the man insisted.

Anger flared in Harriet. "Karl, my schedule is full today. And I don't take bribes."

Some of the people were turning away, but a young woman with a baby in her arms caught at Harriet's sleeve. "My baby is really sick. I'm afraid he'll die."

Harriet looked at the child in her arms. He seemed about eight months old. Even though he was bundled up in a blanket and hat, she could see from his little face that he was pale and way too thin.

"Have you taken him to a doctor?" she asked.

"No. I don't have insurance. I thought maybe … They said if you just touched him …"

The people who had been about to leave turned back and gathered around, their faces expectant. The snow was still falling.

Harriet laid her hand on the baby's head. The Song welled up in her. With a struggle she held it silent. It didn't feel right to begin singing out loud there on the front walk. But with her touch, she saw into his body. He was indeed sick—leukemia. The treatment for that would be impossibly expensive for this woman without insurance. Harriet noted her threadbare coat. And the baby was already far gone.

"He will need more than a touch," Harriet told the mother. "Can you come back at five o'clock?"

The mother nodded.

Harriet turned to the others. "Please leave now. I already have twelve patients today. I do care for all of you, but I am only one woman. Call Brenda for appointments." She gestured again toward the sign on the door.

"You're taking that baby," Karl said.

"I have one appointment a day for an emergency. This child is in critical condition."

"How do you know that?" a middle-aged woman asked.

"I can tell," Harriet answered briefly. She turned to the mother. "What is your name?"

"Margaret Harris."

"All right, Margaret. Take him home now and keep him warm. I'll see you at five."

Conversation was briefly obliterated by the roar of Brenda's motorcycle as she swooped by them down the alley to the parking lot in back.

A moment later she appeared, made her way through the group, and unlocked the door. "Sorry I'm late," she said to Harriet.

Karl stepped up. "You don't understand," he insisted. "My knees are really bad. They hurt so much I can't sleep at night. And I did call. You don't have any openings for six weeks. I need to see you sooner."

"I'm sorry," Harriet said. "I know how difficult pain can be. We'll get you in as soon as we can."

Brenda was scanning the group. "Is one of you Leonard Miller?"

A thin young man leaning on a cane came forward.

"Come on in then," Brenda said, opening the door. "The rest of you, call for an appointment."

"Can't we come in and make an appointment?" a woman asked. "Since we're here?"

"No." Brenda was firm. "I can't have a crowd in the waiting room. We need to keep it quiet so Dr. Ellis can do her work. Call. I'll get back to each of you, I promise. Dr. Ellis will see you as soon as she's available."

Harriet slipped through the open door, followed by Leonard. "Have a seat here," she told him, then fled into her treatment room without even taking off her coat.

She was shaken by the crowd at her door, shaken by the glimpse into the body of the baby boy, and by the effort of holding the Song silent. I'll have to get used to this, she told herself.

She opened the door and called Brenda in.

"Easy, honey," Brenda said, as she helped Harriet out of her coat. "Now where's your lunch? I'll put it in the fridge for you."

"Thanks, Brenda. I want to warn you. I'll be singing out loud from now on. They told me to."

Brenda's eyes widened. "You talked to them?"

"Not exactly. But I got a message." All at once Harriet was smiling with the excitement of what she had to share. "I'll tell you all about it at lunch."

"You'll be singing out loud? Oh, my! How'll I get anything done? I just floated away when I heard you sing for that boy, Jack."

"Maybe you'll get used to it. By the way, a woman with a baby is coming at five o'clock. Margaret Harris. Let her in."

"That'll make thirteen people today," Brenda warned.

"I know. But this baby is really sick."

"You sure have a soft spot for babies. Are you ready for Mr. Miller?"

"Not quite. Start him on filling out an intake form while I catch my breath."

Brenda left. Harriet stood by her treatment table, pressing her hands against her chest, struggling to calm herself. Healing with the Song still felt so strange, as if she were living an alternative life on another planet. After taking seven slow breaths, she let out a long sigh and opened the door.

Leonard had a broken ankle. He'd had surgery three months ago, but it wasn't getting better and he was in a lot of pain. It was hard to get around, even with his cane.

Harriet gestured to him to get up on the table.

"I was snowboarding," he explained, "and I hit a rock sticking out of the snow."

"Ouch," Harriet said, remembering her own collision with the rock on the hillside. "Have you been back to your surgeon?"

"Once," Leonard answered. "But he didn't do anything except tell me to keep wearing this boot." He gestured to the big black boot on his foot and lower leg. "I don't want to go back to him again. I don't trust him. I think he screwed up and doesn't want to cop to it."

"Let's have a look. Can you take off that boot?"

"Yeah. It's a job."

Harriet watched as he began undoing the buckles and Velcro straps. He was young. She glanced over at the intake form on her desk. Eighteen. His hair was a tumble of blond curls, his eyes bright blue. In spite of the pallor from his pain, he shone with the freshness and clarity of youth. Harriet felt a surge of protective tenderness. If Jared had wanted children, she might have had a son this age.

"There," Leonard said as he undid the last strap He winced as he drew the boot off. "I hate this thing. It's heavy and makes me walk weird. And my ankle is still so stiff I can't move my foot around."

Harriet set the boot on the floor and assessed the ankle. It was both swollen and withered from being in the boot so long. The scar was ugly, with red infection around the stitch marks. "I'll be singing as I work," she told Leonard. "It helps the energy flow."

"Like you did for that boy that was written up in the paper?"

"Yes."

"Go for it. Can I watch?"

Harriet nodded. Gently, she cupped his ankle in her hands and released the Song. Its strange, beautiful resonance filled the room. She soon saw that the surgeon had indeed messed up. The leg bone, broken just above the ankle, was not cleanly aligned, and the tendons not well attached. No wonder it didn't heal.

Under her hands, she watched the bone shift into alignment and mend, the tendons attach securely. Then the soft tissue around the ankle filled out and became firm and healthy again. Last of all, the scar and the angry red stitch marks melted away. The Song ended with a sweet, drifting thread of melody. She glanced up at Leonard and saw his eyes round with amazement.

"Cooool!" he exclaimed. "How'd you do that? There's not even a scar!"

Harriet smiled at him. "It should be okay now."

"Awesome!" Leonard exclaimed. "Wow!" He wiggled his foot around. "Wow! Cool! Awesome!"

Before she could stop him, he jumped off the table and stood.

"No pain!" he exclaimed. He looked down at his bare foot, then at the other foot in sock and shoe, and started laughing. "I'm sure not putting that damn boot on again. Guess I'll have to go home with one bare foot."

Harriet laughed with him. "There's snow out there. Maybe you should call a friend."

"Yeah. Hey, thank you. How much do I owe you? That was worth a million, but I don't quite have that."

"Talk to Brenda," Harriet said, opening the door. "Enjoy, and watch out for those rocks."

Leonard bounded out, leaving the boot and his cane behind.

Harriet was happy, the trance still shining in her as she greeted the next patient.

At lunch Harriet told Brenda about the new word, *tirini*, and the messages she had received that morning.

"That's a really good idea," Brenda said, "about keeping one appointment for emergencies. But you are all filled up for six weeks, like that fat man said."

"Then start in six weeks keeping the last one open. Until then I'll take emergencies at five o'clock."

"I told you I'd only schedule twelve people a day for you."

"I'll be all right. The Song gives me strength."

Brenda pressed her lips together and glared. "You're hard to take care of. About you singing aloud," she went on. "Oh, my God, it's beautiful. Makes it hard for me to work. And they stay in the waiting room listening while you sing to the next one. Maybe we should soundproof the wall of the treatment room."

Within a few days, word got around that, if you stood outside the window of Dr. Ellis's office, you could hear her sing, and it was amazing and healing to hear. Most of the day, in spite of the cold, small groups of people lingered there, listening.

Jared

Saturday. Harriet woke to see the first red glow of sunrise out her bedroom window, rolled over and slept again. An hour later, she woke a second time and stretched out with a sigh. At last a day off, nothing scheduled. She could sleep as long as she wanted. As she settled in for another snooze, her phone rang.

"Leave me alone," she grumbled at it, but then rolled over and looked at the extension on her night table. The screen said "Jared."

Jared! She hadn't seen or spoken with him since the day their divorce was final last October.

I can't deal with him this early in the morning, she thought. Let him leave a message.

She turned her back on the phone and burrowed into her pillows. Six rings, and then it was silent. She lay tense in her bed, all impulse for sleep blasted away.

"What the hell does he want?" she muttered. "I don't want to know. I don't want to hear his voice. Ever again. Damn!"

She turned on her side, tried to relax and reclaim her pleasant drowsiness, but it was no use. Thoughts of Jared invaded her.

⌒ ⌒

They had met in a yoga class a year after Harriet came to Denver. Brenda had suggested the class to give her something to do after work, a chance to meet other young people. Harriet enjoyed the class and felt it reinforced some of the things Neal had taught her about standing straight and breathing deeply.

She and Jared were assigned to the back row of the class because they were the tallest. They giggled together at some of the odd poses and glanced at each other with raised eyebrows over some of the woo-woo things the teacher taught them about energy flow.

Then one evening after class, much to Harriet's surprise, Jared asked her out to dinner.

It began as a lighthearted companionship. Jared was a few years older than Harriet, just beginning his law career as a junior partner in a Denver firm. He knew the city and the fun places to go and enjoyed taking her around to theaters, concerts, street festivals, restaurants. They laughed a lot together in those early days.

Before long, their relationship became sexual. Harriet knew she would never love anyone the way she loved Neal, but her summer with Neal had awakened her. Jared was sexy, ardent, and insistent, and after some hesitation she surrendered to the passion he stirred in her.

Then he became possessive and demanding. Still believing herself so unattractive that this might be her only chance for marriage and family, Harriet yielded to his domination. They married a year after they met in a simple ceremony with a justice of the peace.

When Harriet told her family she was married, they were quite upset not to be included. Her mother and sisters put together a reception in the church fellowship hall in Cottonwood Creek attended by everyone Harriet knew, which was almost everyone in Cottonwood Creek. Although Jared was courteous at the reception, Harriet could see he was disdainful of such a hick-town event. The celebration swirled around her. She was the bride, the star, but her heart sank as she began to question the wisdom of her choice.

A year later, Eliza Reilly, fed up with chiropractic, closed her practice. At the same time, Jared was offered a position at a prestigious law firm in Boulder, and Brenda agreed to help Harriet start a new practice there. Jared and Harriet rented an apartment in North Boulder, close to the foothills and the lake. Harriet was delighted to leave the big city and return to the town she had enjoyed as a student.

For a few years, all went well. With Brenda's expert guidance, Harriet's practice grew and thrived, and Jared was a success in the new law firm. Money flowed in, more money than Harriet had ever dreamed of having. She was in her late twenties by then, longing to start a family.

"Not yet," Jared said. Harriet waited.

As his success grew, Jared became more and more obsessed with their image. He insisted she cut her hair and dress more fashionably. Eight years after they moved to Boulder, they bought a house in an upscale North Boulder neighborhood. It had four bedrooms, three baths, an elegant formal living room, a spacious lawn, beautiful landscaping. Plenty big enough for a family.

Harriet was both awed and delighted to have such a home. A week after they moved in, she served their dinner on the patio. She had set the table with candles and flowers from the garden. The summer evening was soft around them. She knew she was ovulating.

"There's lots of room for children in this house," she said as she stroked his thigh in a way she knew excited him.

He pushed her hand away. "No children," he said firmly.

And that was that. She argued, but he was adamant. He didn't want the expense and responsibility. He didn't want to be tied down. He didn't want her to be all involved with babies. He needed her to support him in his career; she was already busy enough with her practice.

She thought of defying him, stopping her birth control pills, but realized it would be cruel to her children to give them a father who didn't want them. So she stuffed her grief and devoted herself to her practice. Her gardens and walks around the lake gave her solace, but the loss remained a cold stone in her gut.

So the years passed.

Then in December of 2009, she fell on the ice and injured her spine, and the sciatic pain began. For a few months Jared was kind and concerned, then became irritated that she didn't get over it, and finally neglected her entirely. Two years later when she was still in a brace following a second spine surgery, he announced abruptly that he wanted a divorce. He also wanted her to move out as soon as possible.

"This is my home," she protested. "You move out if you don't want to live with me anymore."

"You are the one who needs to leave. This house has appreciated in value. You can't afford to buy me out. I can afford to buy you out." Too true. Lawyers make more money than chiropractors, especially soft-hearted ones like her who charged on a sliding scale.

"Don't worry," he added, "You'll have plenty of money to get resettled."

When she protested that it was too soon after her surgery for her to be able to move, he said curtly, "I'll arrange help for you," and left the room.

Within days a real estate agent showed up to take her house hunting and two young women came to help her pack. Three months later, the divorce was final and she was settled in her condo.

The reason for his rush to get her out soon became clear when Cynthia, a sexy, fashionable woman in her thirties, moved into the house with him.

*   *   *

"Damn!" Harriet said again, flinging back the covers and swinging her long legs out of bed. "What can he want? I've half a mind to just erase his message."

She shut her window, pulled on her robe, and turned up the heat.

But of course she was curious. So after putting the tea kettle on, she went back to the bedroom, picked up the phone, and listened to his message.

He had papers he wanted her to sign, something about filing their taxes separately for 2011. Could he stop by?

Stop by? He'd never been to her place. He'd done as he said and arranged help for her move, but he himself had never participated.

She put the phone down and paced. She didn't want to see him. Why couldn't he leave the papers at her office? Brenda could receive them and get them back to him when they were signed. That's what she'd tell him.

The tea kettle whistled. She turned it off and poured herself a big mug of strong English Breakfast tea. While it steeped, she dialed his number. She still knew it by heart.

"This is Harriet," she said when he answered.

"I know. I'd like to come by and have you sign these papers." As always he spoke with authority, without doubt that she would do as he wished.

"I'm busy this morning," she said. "Why don't you drop them by my office on Monday. I'll sign them and Brenda can get them back to you."

"No. I need to get this handled today. Cynthia and I are flying out this evening to the Bahamas."

Cynthia. Harriet's jaw tightened. So now he was taking her to the Bahamas.

"What have you got going on?" Jared asked. "You're there now. I can come right away."

As usual, she wilted before his insistence. "Okay."

"I've got your address. I'll be there in ten." He hung up.

Harriet slammed down the phone. "Why did I just give in?" she muttered. "I'm not even dressed. My tea will be cold. My place is a mess."

She usually kept her little apartment tidy, but she had been weary the night before and left her dishes, thinking she'd have leisure the next morning to clean up. She found herself tensing at the thought of his seeing her untidiness. He had always been so critical.

She strode to her bedroom and threw on some jeans and a sweatshirt, hurried back to the kitchen to have at least a sip of tea while it was still hot, then left her tea to hang up the coat she'd thrown over a chair the night before.

He'd be there any minute. It was only a half mile from the lovely house that had once been her home to the humbler neighborhood where her condo was.

Her hair. She hadn't combed her hair. But the doorbell rang before she could get to it.

He stood in the doorway, tall and suave, glancing over her living room, her kitchenette with the dirty dishes, her baggy sweatshirt, her rumpled hair. A half smile touched his lips.

"So this is your place? It's small. I gave you more than half a million, and this is what you got?"

"I saved most of it," she said. "I didn't think I could work much longer with the back pain. But I'm better now."

Why did she always have to explain herself to him? It was none of his business.

"I heard you were better. Glad to hear it." He came in, settled on her couch, and opened his briefcase. "Sign here and here," he said as he spread some papers out on the coffee table. "Jodi has the rest of the paperwork. You can go by at your convenience. Starting this year, I'm moving my affairs to a more sophisticated accountant, one familiar with a more complex business structure. You'll probably want to stay with Jodi. She's adequate for your business."

"Yes, she is." Harriet liked Jodi and had no intention of changing accountants. *He acts so damn superior,* she thought. *How did I stand it for thirty years?* She could guess what Jared's "more sophisticated accountant" would be. Someone expert in tax avoidance.

She sat down and looked over the papers. They were pretty straightforward, stating that she agreed to separate their taxes for 2011. She signed.

"Thanks," Jared said, as he slipped the papers back into his briefcase.

He frowned at her. "What's this I hear about you singing to your patients? There was an article in the paper last week. And now I hear people are standing outside your office window, listening. Tying up parking and traffic. What the hell are you doing?"

"I've found that if I sing to my patients, it helps the healing."

"That's crazy woo-woo stuff. Have you gone off the deep end?"

How could he still make her feel so wrong and small?

She drew in her breath and lifted her head. "It works. Some of my patients have had miraculous healings. Did you read the article in the paper? Even the doctors were amazed."

"Miraculous healings!" His voice was rich with scorn. "Who do you think you are? Jesus Christ?"

"No." Harriet was shaken.

"It's embarrassing for me, people thinking I was married so long to a kook."

Harriet stood up. "I'm sorry for you," she said coldly. "Be glad you're not married to me anymore. I certainly am."

She strode to the door and opened it. "It's time for you to go."

A startled look crossed Jared's face. She had never stood up to him before. He picked up his briefcase, hesitated at the door.

"Goodbye," Harriet said.

"Goodbye." He left.

Harriet shut the door behind him. A rush of triumph coursed through her. I kicked him out, she gloated inwardly. Why didn't I think of that twenty-five years ago?

She went back to the table in her breakfast nook. Her tea was cold. Her brief moment of elation at the look on Jared's face when she showed him the door crumpled into doubt.

His words, "Who do you think you are? Jesus Christ?" reverberated in her.

Who *did* she think she was? Why had the Song been given to her? She wasn't anybody. She wasn't worthy.

Maybe she *was* a kook.

All the peace of her day was shattered. She dropped into her chair, pushed her tea aside, and laid her head on her arms.

February

February came in with a big snowstorm, then another. But after that the air softened, the days lengthened, and Harriet began to feel the promise of imminent spring. It would be truly spring for her, after the long winter of pain and grief that had lasted two years in spite of outward season changes. Each day she woke with gratitude for her healing.

Her practice was moving along relatively smoothly. Brenda had the ability to be both firm and compassionate. Gradually word got around, and Harriet's would-be patients understood they must wait for an appointment. Still there was a cluster at the door each morning and stiff competition for the one emergency appointment a day. And there was almost always a group hovering outside her window to hear her sing. She frequently got requests for interviews. Brenda turned them all down firmly, but occasionally Harriet found it necessary to escape through the back window at the end of the day.

There had been no more revelations from the bubbles since she'd received the idea of the emergency appointment, the odd word, *tirini*, and the instruction to sing aloud; but often in her dreams she heard their singing, and during the day, as she healed with the Song, she felt them with her. Spending so many hours each day in the love and ecstasy of the Song was changing her subtly, washing away the pain and sorrow that, hidden, had been part of her all her life. She was still tall and bony, her features still angular, her nose still large, but her face, with her wide green eyes, began to shine with a quality of beauty that transcended physical features.

Brenda was absolutely adamant that Harriet not work on weekends, so she had two days at home each week. She had always been introverted and had no friends except Brenda, who spent her weekends cruising with her motorcycle buddies and visiting her family. During Harriet's marriage to Jared, all their social life had revolved around his career, and once they were divorced, she was completely dropped from his circle. Her patients adored her, but something in her reserve kept them from daring to offer friendship.

So she spent her weekends quietly alone, resting, reading, walking in the foothills. Sometimes she felt lonely, but mostly she was glad for quiet time after the intensity of the week.

She didn't miss the big house she'd shared with Jared as much as she'd thought she would, but she did miss the garden. One Saturday morning, she stood looking out her back door, feeling the strengthening sun on her face and dreaming of what she might do with her pocket-sized backyard and the little patch of earth by her front door.

Although she had been dazed with pain, grief, and anger when she'd gone house hunting the summer before, she'd known that she would need some earth and had insisted on a ground floor apartment. She was so glad now that she had.

Some roses, she thought, one on each side of the front door. And maybe in back, a couple of tomato plants and some greens. And some low-growing flowers like lobelia and sweet alyssum to plant along the front walkway. She remembered seeing some seed racks in the hardware store the last time she'd been there. It was a early still, but maybe she could get some seeds and plant them in trays on her south window sill.

Excited by her idea, she went to get her purse and coat. She stopped by the bathroom to run a comb through her hair.

It looks awful, she thought. All ragged. She fussed with it a little. Her hair had always been thick and grown fast, and she hadn't had it cut since the divorce. The shortest parts now hung as low as her ear lobes. There were gray streaks near her brow, but most of it was still the rich brown color it had always been.

I should get a trim, she thought, get it evened up, shaped a little. Still feeling the sense of springtime coming, she decided. I'll do it today after I pick up the seeds. There's a walk-in place right near the hardware store.

The hairdresser in the walk-in beauty shop was a man, probably in his fifties, with thick dark hair and a warm smile.

"I want to grow it out," Harriet told him. "It used to hang to my waist. Can you shape it so it looks okay in the process?"

"Sure I can." He ran his fingers through her hair, lifted and shook it. "Good hair."

His fingers in her hair.

She closed her eyes as he began to cut, swept back to a Saturday morning in Neal's office the summer before she went to college.

⮵ ⮴

He came up behind her as she sat at her desk and ran his fingers through her long, loose hair.

"In a month you're going to college," he said. "I've been wondering if you'd like to try another hairdo. I have an idea. May I?"

"May you what?"

"Fix it for you."

She turned in surprise to look up at him. "You? Do you know how to fix hair?"

"I'd like to try."

She blushed. "Okay."

"Where's your hairbrush?"

She opened the desk drawer and handed it to him. Gently, he began to brush, smoothing her hair back from her temples, her ears. Liquid fire rose from her loins, spreading its warmth all through her body. Just his touch, she thought, and I melt. She'd always especially loved the way he touched her hair.

"So beautiful," he said. "It's like shining silk. Don't ever cut it."

He laid down the brush, gathered her hair up in his hands, bent, and kissed the curve of her neck. Then he braided until all her hair was confined in a thick, long plait.

She thought he would stop there and started to stand up, but he put his hand on her shoulder. "No wait. I'm not done."

She felt him twisting the braid up, shaping it somehow on the back of her neck, securing it with something.

"What are you doing?" She twisted in the chair.

"Hold still. I'm creating a chignon." He pronounced the word with an exaggerated French accent.

Harriet began to giggle.

"But what are you holding it with?"

"I went shopping. Hair pins. And we'll decorate it with this." He showed her a comb, edged with mother-of-pearl in a delicate, scroll-like pattern.

"Where did you get that?" she asked. "It's beautiful. I never saw anything like that at Woolworth's."

"I never did either. I got it up in Parker. If I'd bought anything here at Woolworth's, Nellie Olson would take note, and tongues would wag the first time you wore it. Now let me finish."

She felt him press the comb into the side of the twist and put her hand back to feel the shape of all her hair gathered in one place.

Neal tipped his head to one side, smiling at her. "Come have a look." He led her to the bathroom where she could see herself in the mirror.

He had draped her hair in a soft wave by her cheek before gathering it back. She looked elegant, mature.

"What do you think?" he asked.

"It's really different." She hesitated, turning her head to look at the side view. "But I like it. I'll wear it this way now. I think I can learn to fix it okay." She put her arms around him, hugged him, and kissed him. "Thank you for the beautiful comb."

Then the hairdo got rather messed up, but later she had the opportunity to fix it herself, with him guiding her.

She had worn her hair that way for years. Until Jared said she looked too much like a hippie and insisted she cut it.

Over the years she'd bought other combs to adorn her twist of braid and, after her haircut, had kept them hidden in the bottom of her jewelry box in silent defiance of Jared. But none was as dear to her as the mother-of-pearl comb Neal gave her that day. Now, maybe in a year or so, her hair would be long enough that she could wear it again.

Chapter 16

Fifty-fifth Birthday

Harriet's birthday, February 25, was on a Saturday that year. During her regular call home the week before, her mother had said, "Come down for your birthday. We'll give you a party on Saturday night. We miss you."

"That would be nice," Harriet said. "I'll come. But, Mom, not a big party. Please. You know how I am. Just a little party with family. Could Emma come down? I haven't seen her for years."

"I'll call Emma," her mother answered. "I bet she can come now that Lillian's in college. It will be wonderful to have all three of my girls here. Bring that pretty, green velvet dress you wore last time you came down."

The following Friday, Harriet was on the road again in late afternoon traffic, her green dress swaying on a hanger in the back window. No snow this time. The sky was clear and the waxing moon just setting as she arrived in Cottonwood Creek and turned down the quiet streets toward her parents' home.

Her mother had roasted a chicken with all the fixings. As they sat down to eat together, Harriet studied her parents. Her mother looked better, with more color in her face than she'd had the month before. Her father looked much worse. His skin was sallow, his eyes dull, and he moved with difficulty. Harriet remembered her brief glimpse into his body on her last visit, before his resistance had shut down the Song— the clogged coronal arteries, the sickness in his liver.

He's bad off, she thought. I wish he'd let me help him. I'll try again. But she didn't have much hope he would let her.

Her mother chattered excitedly about plans for the party. Emma was coming down from Colorado Springs, and of course Sophie and Mary and Jimmy would be there with their families. And Reverend Harvey was coming. And—the list grew.

Harriet's heart sank. "Mom, I told you I wanted only a small party. Just family."

Her mother fluttered her hands. "But they all wanted to be invited when they heard you were coming down, and that it's your fifty-fifth. Everyone wants to see you because you sang so beautifully the last time you were here."

"Oh, Mom."

"It'll be fine, honey. You mustn't be so shy. We're all so proud of you."

Harriet bent her head. The old habit was always stronger here in Cottonwood Creek, and her hair was beginning to be long enough to fall forward and shield her face. But she shouldn't duck like that. She wasn't a child anymore. She took a deep breath and lifted her head.

Her mother's face was all lit up with the excitement of the party. And Reverend Harvey. I mustn't disappoint her, Harriet thought. I can deal.

"That's a lot of people to fit in this house," she said.

"Yes. Too many. Reverend Harvey said we can use the fellowship hall at the church. And Reverend Harvey wants you to sing again on Sunday."

"Oh!" Harriet swallowed.

"You will, won't you?"

Harriet struggled inwardly with her discomfort at being noticed. She remembered the sweetness of sharing the Song's love through a hymn and the feeling of the hushed congregation receiving it. She knew it had been a gift to them. How could she refuse?

"Okay," she said. "But I need to talk with Reverend Harvey about what hymn he wants."

"He's coming to call on you tomorrow."

Her father, who had been sitting slumped in his chair throughout the whole conversation, spoke up. "Your mother gets all excited whenever the pastor comes to call." There was irony in his voice and in the quick glance he gave his wife.

Harriet hastened to turn the conversation. "How are you doing, Dad?"

"As well as can be expected."

"And the store? The business?"

"A little slow this time of year, but folks do come in." He took a sip from his gin and tonic and subsided into silence.

Later that evening, after the dishes were cleaned up, Harriet went to her father who had retired to his chair beside the stove with a fresh drink. She pulled a chair up beside him and laid a hand on his knee. "It's good to see you again, Dad."

As soon as she touched him, the Song rose up in full force and she got a glimpse into his body. It was bad. Everything she'd seen on her last visit was worse. He pushed her hand away, and the Song rebounded with such force that she gasped.

"What're you doing?" he asked irritably. "You gave me a shock. Must've been scuffing the rug up when you came over here."

"Sorry," Harriet said, rubbing her rejected hand. For a brief moment, the old childhood grief assailed her. Her shoulders tightened. No matter how hard she tried, nothing she did pleased her father. Then grief was replaced with alarm. He'll die soon, she thought, if something isn't done.

Her mother came into the room with a photo album. "Come here, Harrie. I want to show you this album Sophie put together of Harry and Timmy and Jenny. She's taken such cute pictures. She takes them with her telephone, digitally, she says. There's no film. Can you imagine?"

Releasing her shoulders with a brief shudder, Harriet turned away from her father, went to sit on the couch beside her mother, and put an arm around her.

The Song rose up. She pressed it down, but not before she saw a new tumor beginning to grow in her mother's lung. For a moment she struggled with the Song. She withdrew her arm. Not now, she told it. Later. It subsided. Harriet sat still in surprise. Can I control when the Song comes? she wondered.

Her mother had opened the album and was talking, but Harriet couldn't follow her. She was dealing with the sight of the new tumor where only a month ago the Song had banished the old tumor and created a clean, healthy lung. Why is it coming back? she asked herself. Doesn't the healing last?

"And look at this," Harriet's mother was saying. "That little Jenny is *so* cute. Look at that smile."

Harriet wrestled herself out of her confusion and brought her attention to the pictures. "She has a great smile. Is that a tooth?"

"Yes. It's her first tooth. And I love this picture of the boys. What a pair!"

After they had looked at all the pictures, Harriet put her arm around her mother again. "It's been a long day," she said. "I want to go up to bed soon, but first I'd like to sing to you a little. I have a special song for you. May I?"

"Oh, honey, I'd love that."

She laid her head on Harriet's shoulder. Softly, Harriet began to sing. The Song's love and Harriet's love for her mother blended, and gradually the new tumor faded away.

As she sang, Harriet scanned the rest of her mother's body. The bones were still strong and the heart still steady. But the tumor—why had it come back? Even though it was gone again now, Harriet felt afraid. If it came back and she weren't there to sing it away, her mother might die, too.

Later, up in her room, Harriet thought, I must try to ask them. How can I? What if I just say that word. Maybe they'll answer. She hadn't tried that before.

Sitting still on the edge of her bed, she called softly, "Eliria."

Immediately she felt a response, a rush of energy, a tingling throughout her body, a sense of presence.

"The tumor came back," she told the presence. "Why did it come back? Doesn't the healing last? I can't be with my mother all the time to sing it away again." A rush of grief and fear clogged her throat. "What do I need to do to make it last? She's my mother. Do you understand?"

Song rose inside her, a soft, comforting Song. *Ah*, they seemed to sing. It was so loving, so soothing that Harriet calmed.

"Why did it come back?" she asked again.

Then it seemed that the Song rose and wove in a questioning way, as if several voices were asking each other her question. Then one voice, a deep rich voice, seemed to sing, *We don't know.*

"You don't know!" Harriet exclaimed. "Then who does know?"

Ah, the voices sang, then faded away.

❧ ❦

The next morning Harriet went to the store to pick up a few things for her mother. The Cottonwood Creek grocery was the same as always, the aisles narrow, the wood floor slightly warped so the cart bumped as Harriet pushed it along.

She had almost finished gathering the items on her mother's list, when she rounded a corner and met Neal's daughter, Nan.

Both of Neal's children had been well educated and returned to live in Cottonwood Creek, Nan to teach elementary school and Roger to become the town lawyer.

"Happy birthday, Harrie," Nan greeted her. "How nice to see you. We're looking forward to your party tonight." Nan was pretty. She looked like Neal, the same blue eyes and light brown, wavy hair.

"It's nice to see you, too. You know about my party? Are you and Henry coming?

"We sure are. It's going to be fun. Mike's three-piece band is going to play for the dancing, and Angie—remember Angie, my youngest?—is going to babysit the little kids so the grown-ups can relax."

"Oh." Harriet gulped. "I didn't know it was going to be such a big deal." She felt herself shrinking inside.

"You're gifting us," Nan said, laughing. "It's great to have an occasion for a party. It can get kind of dull around here, especially in the winter."

Harriet took a deep breath. "I was sorry to hear about your mother passing last summer."

Nan sobered. "We miss her. Everyone does. She was such a sociable person, kind of the center of everything. The quilting circle just fell apart after she died."

"I'm sure she's missed," Harriet said. "My mother really enjoyed the quilting circle." She hesitated, then asked, "How is your father? Last time I was here, Roger told me he was ill, away in California for treatment." Harriet realized she was pressing her hand to her heart and quickly dropped it to her side.

"Not good," Nan said. "I went out to visit him a couple of weeks ago. It's a nice place where he is. They take good care of him. But he's faded terribly since the last time I saw him. I don't know if they're really helping him. He's clearly well loved there. Lot's of people spoke to me to tell me—"

She stopped speaking as quick tears came to her eyes. "*You* know," she said, reaching out to touch Harriet's hand, "how kind and wise he is. You worked for him long ago. I remember, even though I was just a kid at the time, that folks said you had a big crush on him."

Harriet caught her breath. "I didn't know they said that. I was … fond of him. He inspired me."

"I'm sure he did." Nan said. "He's really missed here. We've no doctor in Cottonwood Creek now. People keep asking about him, hoping he'll get well and start his practice again. But, short of a miracle, I don't see how he can. We need a doctor in town. Did you ever think about coming home and opening a practice here?"

It took a moment for Harriet to answer, as memories swirled. Then she said carefully, "No, as long as Neal was here, there wasn't need."

"Well, there's need now. You should consider it." Nan smiled and touched Harriet's hand again. "I've got to run. See you tonight."

"You look different," Emma said. She tilted her head to one side, studying Harriet. "Your hair is longer. Are you growing it out again? But that's not it." She paused, tilted her head to the other side. "It's your eyes. They're greener than they used to be. Are you wearing colored contacts?"

Emma and Sophie had arrived around noon and greeted Harriet warmly. The three sisters were gathered in the kitchen helping their mother fix lunch.

"I noticed that, too," Sophie said, "the last time you came down. I was going to ask you about your eyes, but the kids were making so much commotion I didn't get to it. What have you done to them? They look great. And your hair looks better, too."

Harriet turned to smile at Sophie, grateful for her noticing and appreciating the changes in her appearance.

Emma had grown stout over the last few years and dyed her hair blond. Now she persisted. "*Are* you wearing contacts?"

"No," Harriet answered.

"Then what did you do to your eyes? They never used to be such a pretty color."

"Harrie always had pretty eyes," their mother said.

That's mother love for you, Harriet thought. They were never pretty before I received the Song. She had almost forgotten how her eyes used to be until Emma brought it up.

"Maybe it was all the drugs you had to take for your surgeries," Sophie suggested. "Those drugs can do weird things to people."

"Lunch is ready. Come sit down," their mother said.

As they ate, their mother laid out plans for the party. Then Emma talked non-stop about her three children, all in college now. She was funny and articulate and soon had them laughing.

Harriet watched her mother. She's happy, Harriet thought. Glad to have all her daughters together.

⁓ ⁓

The party was in full swing. The fellowship hall was decorated with crepe paper and balloons, the band was playing, the young people dancing. Harriet sat at a table with her parents and her sisters. After dreading the party all day, Harriet found, to her surprise, that she was having fun. All evening friends and neighbors had been coming to her, complimenting her, hugging her, congratulating her. She felt warm and bubbly inside. This is why people like being the center of attention, she realized with amazement.

Dulce, Sophie's housekeeper, was setting out refreshments on a long table at the end of the hall by the kitchen. Her two young boys were helping her, and her youngest child, a little girl of about two, all dressed up in a red velvet dress, was dancing, whirling around and around by the kitchen door.

Harriet watched her, delighting in the child's light, lively grace. "Dulce's little girl is adorable," she said to Sophie.

"Her name's Lucia," Sophie said. "She's precious."

The band wound up the boisterous piece they were playing and started a quieter one, a waltz.

"Would you like to dance?" Reverend Harvey stood by the table, holding out his hand to Harriet.

"Oh, my!" Harriet's mother gasped. "She'd love to, wouldn't you, Harrie?"

Harriet blushed. Sometimes her mother …

She resisted the temptation to duck her head. "Thank you," she said, smiling at Reverend Harvey. She stood, tall and elegant in her green velvet dress, and took his hand. She did know how to dance; she and Jared had taken ballroom lessons as part of polishing their social skills. But it had been long ago.

Reverend Harvey danced well, guiding her skillfully around the floor, and gradually Harriet relaxed. She'd forgotten how much fun it was to dance.

Just as the song was ending, there was a crash over by the kitchen door, then screaming—the terrible screaming of a child in pain.

The band stopped playing. Everyone rushed toward the sound. The floor in front of the refreshment table was spattered with broken crockery, chicken pieces, and oil. Dulce knelt in the middle of it, holding Lucia in her arms.

Harriet cut through the crowd. Reverend Harvey was beside her. "Move back," he ordered. "Harriet's a doctor. Give her room."

"What happened?" Harriet asked, bending over Dulce.

"She ran into me while I was carrying the chicken, knocked it out of my hands, and it spilt all over her. Hot oil," Dulce sobbed.

Harriet could barely hear her over Lucia's screams. She laid her hand on Dulce's shoulder. "Quick. Bring her to the kitchen. Cold water." She turned to her sister. "Sophie, help us."

Dulce understood and got up, her child in her arms, and hurried to the kitchen. Sophie followed.

Reverend Harvey, asked, "What can I do?"

"Close the door."

Harriet strode to the sink and turned on the cold water. Dulce thrust Lucia under it. Lucia gasped with the shock and stopped screaming.

Harriet held out her hands. "May I take her?"

Dulce handed her the child. The moment Harriet touched her, the Song rose. "Ah," she sang, as the voices had sung to her. Lucia turned her head and looked up at Harriet with her big dark eyes, her breath coming in gasping sobs. Harriet struggled, needing to speak to the child, to her mother, but not wanting to stop the Song. *Let the Song come through my words*, she prayed, and found that she could speak and still feel the energy of the Song pouring silently through her.

"You're going to be okay," Harriet said to the child. Inside she felt as if she were juggling with too many balls in the air—keeping the Song silent when it was so needed in full force, comforting Dulce and Lucia, and somehow keeping them from knowing the truth about the Song.

She turned to Sophie. "Are there towels in this kitchen?"

Sophie opened a drawer and brought a pile of towels to Harriet. Lucia's sobs had subsided, but she was pale and shivering.

"We need to get her wet dress off and get her warm," Harriet said. "Is there a blanket anywhere we could wrap her in?"

"I think there's one in our donation box," Sophie said. "I'll get it." She hurried out.

Gently, Harriet and Dulce eased Lucia out of her dress, revealing the delicate, little brown body and the searing burn across her chest. Bad burns, Harriet could see, covering the whole right side of her face and neck and most of her chest. The Song rose stronger.

Sophie returned with the blanket. Harriet pulled up an old chair from the corner of the kitchen, took Lucia in her lap, and wrapped her in the blanket. She turned to Sophie and Dulce, "Now, soak those towels in cold water and lay them on the burns. The cold water will heal the burns. I'm going to sing to her to calm her." She hated to put cold water on Lucia again, but it was the only way she knew to cover up what she was really doing. Wrapping the blanket close around the child, Harriet let go into the Song, sending warmth through her hands as she laid them gently over the cold towels.

"Hot oil," Dulce sobbed as she worked, "all over her face. She'll be scarred for life."

"Hush," Harriet said, as the Song poured through her. "The cold water will heal her. We got it in time."

"I seen that kind of burn before," Dulce moaned. "Cold water's not enough."

"Hush," Harriet said again. "She will heal."

For the next half hour she sang to Lucia while Sophie and Dulce changed the cold compresses. Each time they lifted the towels, the burns were lighter. Dulce and Sophia glanced at each other, wonder in their faces. Lucia looked up at Harriet, trusting, throughout the process, and finally closed her eyes.

"She's dropping off," Harriet said. "I think we can stop the compresses now."

The band was playing again. "I left an awful mess out there," Dulce said, "and who knows what my boys are up to."

"I'll sit with her awhile longer," Harriet said. "You go on and look after your boys. Is there a quiet place where she can rest while you clean up?"

"Reverend Harvey's office," Sophie said. "I'll ask him."

In the privacy of Reverend Harvey's office, Harriet was able to sing freely, without having to speak or be concerned about what anyone thought. Lucia's little body was warm and soft in her arms, the Song incredibly sweet as it worked through the last layers of the burns, restoring healthy tissue and smooth, brown skin. Harriet felt her tension melting away. She nestled the child closer and drifted in the ecstasy of the Song.

There was a knock on the door. Sophie peeked in. "Can you come now? Dulce's on her way up to get Lucia. We've got everything cleaned up and they want to give you your birthday cake."

☙ ❧

The next afternoon, Harriet walked through the quiet streets of Cottonwood Creek toward the manse. Reverend Harvey had invited her to tea again. "I'd like to catch up with you," he'd said to her before the Sunday service.

She had sung in church that morning. The love of the Song had flowed through her hymn, and the congregation had been as hushed and entranced as they had been the first time. After the service, she'd run away again, out the back door and down the alley. All the attention she had received the night before at her birthday party was plenty.

But she was looking forward to talking with Reverend Harvey. She felt confused and upset about her mother's new tumor and the whole event with Lucia. She longed to confide in him, trusting his gentle wisdom.

Even so, she hesitated on the porch of the manse, suddenly shy, remembering dancing with him the night before. She took a deep breath, and rang the doorbell.

Reverend Harvey welcomed her warmly. "Come in, Harriet. Would you like peppermint tea again?

"Yes, thank you," Harriet answered. "You know," she said as he hung up her coat, "I really appreciate that you always remember to call me Harriet, even when everyone else around here calls me Harrie."

"Oh, I understand," he said. "With a name like Winston. They used to call me Winnie when I was a boy. You can imagine what that led to on the playground."

Harriet laughed. "I can guess."

Soon they were seated in his comfortable living room with tea.

"I've thought of you so often over the last month," he said, "still marveling at your story and wondering if you've managed to communicate with your bubbles."

"A little," Harriet said, and went on to tell him of the words *eliria* and *tirini* and the advice that she sing aloud and save an emergency appointment each day. "And last night …"

"Tell me about last night. What happened in the kitchen after I closed the door? We could hear you singing. People just wanted to stand and listen, but someone got the band going again, and you were drowned out."

"Just as well," Harriet said.

"The child looked fine when Dulce carried her out. No sign of a burn."

"No, the Song healed the burns. They were bad. I was so glad I was there. She's a beautiful child. I'd have hated to see her scarred."

Harriet drew in her breath, awed anew at the gift of the Song, remembering the bright grace of Lucia's dancing, the warm, sweet weight of her in her lap.

"But one part was hard," she said. "I felt like I had to hide what was really happening. I had Dulce and Sophie put cold compresses on her while I sang, and pretended the cold compresses were what healed the burns. It would have been better just to sing. Lucia was in shock and the cold made her shiver more. And I don't think my pretense worked anyway."

"Why do you think you have to pretend?"

"Because it's so strange. I'm afraid people will think I'm weird. Like my former husband. He said he was ashamed to have been married to such a kook. And also, if word gets out, I'll be inundated, like in Boulder. This is my safe place to run to where no one knows."

Reverend Harvey nodded. "I understand."

Harriet twisted her fingers together in her lap. "There's something else that happened. With my mother."

"Tell me."

Harriet told him about healing her mother during her last visit and that she'd found a new tumor when she returned. "I'm scared," she said. "The Song healed it, but what if it comes back and I'm not here to sing it away? Why do you think it came back?"

Reverend Harvey rubbed his chin. "The tumor is a symptom. If the underlying cause is not addressed, the symptom will come back. I'm sure you know that."

"I do." Harriet felt a shift within herself. "Thank you for reminding me. I've been thinking like a child scared of losing her mother, forgetting what I know as a doctor."

"So, what do you think lies behind the recurring tumor?" Reverend Harvey asked. "I haven't seen your mother smoke."

"Oh, no. Never." Harriet frowned. "I don't think she's very happy. My father … he's never been affectionate or appreciative. Now he's more grumpy and demanding than ever. She waits on him hand and foot. That's her life. It's good that Jimmy and Sophie and Mary and the great grandchildren are here. They brighten her up, but they're busy and don't get by often."

"Was she part of the quilting circle? I've heard that was an important part of the lives of a number of women in town who are at loose ends since Sarah Walker died."

Harriet shivered. It was so hard to believe Sarah was dead—and Neal dying. If only he were not so far away. She pulled herself together. Reverend Harvey was still talking.

"Maybe it would be good to get that circle started up again. Do you think your mother might take it on? It would give her a project."

"She's kind of shy," Harriet said. "But she could. She's got good organizational skills. After all, she raised three daughters, did the bookkeeping for the shoe store, and always kept our home in good order."

"I'll call on her and suggest it. Maybe I could help her set it up."

"She'd love that. She's got quite a crush on you, you know. I bet she's not the only one."

Reverend Harvey's cheeks flushed. Harriet caught a glimpse of another side of him. Maybe he, like Harriet, was shy underneath.

He shrugged, then grinned at her. "It's an occupational hazard."

Driving back to Boulder that evening, Harriet mulled over her conversation with Reverend Harvey. Of course the symptoms come back when the underlying cause is not addressed. All those people that the Song healed—had it reached the cause or only relieved the symptoms? Celia? Maybe it hadn't yet gotten to the cause with her. Leonard with the broken ankle—the Song probably got to the bottom of that one. She remembered how the scar had just faded away.

Harriet shook her head and focused on the road. She was leaving the two-lane highway and merging onto I-70. Once she'd settled into the lane she would stay in until she reached Denver, her thoughts turned back to her afternoon with Reverend Harvey. Her heart warmed as she thought of him, his quiet compassion, his wisdom, and that moment when she'd glimpsed his shyness. He's so kind, she thought, to think of a way to help Mom. Mom will love it. She'll start up the quilting circle again just to have him help her. And it will be good for her, a project, like he said.

She thought of his warm, blue eyes, the way he grinned when she teased him, the way he'd danced with her. I could get a crush on him, too. Better not.

Chapter 17

Cottonwood Creek Visits

After her birthday, Harriet drove down to Cottonwood Creek a couple of times a month. She was happy to connect with her family again after the two long years of not being able to drive that far.

She checked her mother every time she visited. There were no new tumors. True to his word, Reverend Harvey had helped her revive the quilting circle, and her mother was busy with her new project, happier than Harriet had seen her in years.

With each visit, Harriet became increasingly concerned about her father; but every time she touched him, he snapped at her and the Song bounced back. Finally she gave up trying.

She was especially eager to renew her relationship with Sophie, but there was a slight uneasiness between them. Harriet suspected Sophie knew she was hiding something and was hurt that Harriet didn't confide in her, but Harriet didn't know how to bring up the subject or what she could possibly say.

One weekend Sophie invited her out to the ranch. It was warm for April. They sat in afternoon sunshine on the back porch overlooking the plains. A soft green was beginning to emerge from the brown grasses. Harriet felt her body soften with the peace that always came to her when she opened to the vastness of the plains and the immensity of the sky above.

Dulce, with Lucia following her, brought them tea and cookies. Lucia ran to Harriet, holding up her arms. "Sing?" she asked. Her face was shining with joy and welcome.

Harriet held out her arms, glad to see Lucia looking so beautiful and well. She gathered the little girl into her lap.

"Sing?" Lucia asked again.

Harriet didn't know what to do. She wanted to sing to Lucia to assure herself that all was well with her. Sophie was watching her intently, but Harriet couldn't bear to refuse the child. "Is it all right if I sing to her a little bit?" she asked Dulce.

"Si, Señora!" Dulce clasped her hands together over her heart. "Your song is a miracle, a blessing from God. Singing away her burns like you did."

Harriet took another quick glance at Sophie.

"We'd love it if you'd sing," Sophie said.

Harriet drew Lucia closer, cherishing the sweetness of the small, delicate body nestled against her bosom. She felt the Song rise and her vision open. Lucia was perfectly healthy. At first it seemed there was no need for the Song except that Lucia wanted it. Then Harriet realized there was still trauma. The burns were gone, but not the shock.

The Song came softly, full of tenderness. Lucia's little body melted into Harriet as the tension from the shock dissolved. Lost in the trance and the love she felt for Lucia, Harriet had no idea how long she sang. When the Song faded away, Lucia was asleep in her arms and Dulce was kneeling by her chair, tears on her cheeks. Sophia was sitting opposite Harriet, her face soft, her eyes questioning.

Dulce got up stiffly. "Shall I take her, Señora?"

Harriet looked down at Lucia. "She's asleep. I love holding her."

Dulce nodded, and went back through the kitchen door.

"It's a shame you never had kids of your own," Sophie said. "You're so good with them."

Harriet felt the old lump of grief in her throat. "I'm so grateful you shared yours with me."

Sophie learned forward in her chair. "Harrie, what's really going on? Dulce and I both know it wasn't the cold compresses that healed

Lucia's burns. They were way too bad. Dulce thinks you are an angel. I know better than that." She gave Harriet an affectionate smile. "But something's happened to you. You were gone for two years, got divorced, Mom said you were in a lot of pain and having surgeries that didn't work. Then you came back. You're fine. No pain. Mary's still marveling about that time last winter when Jenny, who was really sick, got perfectly well all at once while you were holding her. And your singing. You've always had a nice voice, but you never used to sing the way you do now. Even your eyes are different."

Harriet felt like a child caught with her hand in the cookie jar— found out, embarrassed, almost ashamed. She didn't know how to respond. She bent her head. "Please don't talk about it," she said finally.

"Why?"

"Because … you know how this town is. Everyone will think I'm weird. They already do. They always have."

"What? You're nuts. Remember your birthday party? Everyone getting together to celebrate you? How the church is packed every time you sing? It's true you were kind of an odd kid, but you're grown up now and all the kids who called you weird have grown up, too. Now they admire you."

Sophie reached out to touch Harriet's knee. "Please share with me. I won't tell anyone if you don't want me to, but I'm your sister. I want to understand. Why won't you tell me?"

"Because I don't *know* what happened. I'm still trying to figure it out." Harriet took a deep breath. "Okay. I'll tell you what I do know. Last January I took a walk at night, cut across a frozen lake, and fell through the ice. I should have died, but someone rescued me. I have no clue who. When I came to, I was healed of my sciatic pain and was singing, like I do now. Then I found out that the Song could heal others. I started using it in my practice. And now it's gotten crazy because everyone wants to be healed. Of course. They crowd the door of my office and hang out outside my window to listen to me sing. But I can't heal them all. I'm only one woman. So I come down here to get away."

Sophie's face had paled. "You fell through the ice? What on earth were you doing? You shouldn't be walking alone at night."

Harriet didn't know how to answer. She surely wasn't going to tell Sophie about her suicide attempt.

Sophie was bursting with questions. "You don't know who rescued you? How you got healed? I'm glad *someone* pulled you out. What could have happened—to heal you, to change your eyes, to give you singing that heals?"

"I don't know."

"No idea?"

"Some ideas, but I can't make much sense of them. I'm just incredibly grateful to be out of pain and able to help others. But it's a huge responsibility. Don't you see? A gift and also a burden."

"I get it. I won't talk. Can you heal anything?"

"It's not me; it's the Song. Yes, it can heal anything."

"Can it heal Dad? I'm worried about him."

"I'm worried about him, too. But he won't let the Song in. He won't let me touch him. I've tried. The Song is able to help Mom."

Sophie nodded. "I've noticed that she's much better since you started visiting again. I thought you might have had something to do with that." She hesitated. "Do you think the Song could heal the arthritis in my knees?"

"I know it could."

"Would you?"

Harriet got up slowly and laid the sleeping child on the porch swing. Going to her sister, she knelt in front of her, put her hands on Sophie's knees, and began to sing.

⌒ ⌒

Every time she went home, Harriet sang in church. Word would go out through the small-town network, and the sanctuary would be packed. Harriet began to be braver about not running away after the service, but still felt awkward and didn't know what to say when people pressed around to tell her how her singing had touched them.

Reverend Harvey always invited her for a visit on Sunday afternoon. Harriet began to look forward to her time with him as one of the best parts of her trips to Cottonwood Creek.

She delighted in his subtle humor, his friendly companionship, and most of all in their conversations. Sometimes they sat in his parlor with tea, and sometimes, as the weather grew warmer, they walked together by the creek.

For their walks, he wore a green felt baseball cap with the capital letters PTL embroidered in white script across the front. The hat and the angle at which he wore it tickled Harriet. It didn't fit in with her experience of ministerial charisma.

"What does PTL stand for?" she'd asked him.

He'd glanced over at her with a mischievous smile. "Praise The Lord."

Harriet couldn't help giggling. "That's unique."

"Get the Word out anyway you can," he'd said, laughing with her.

In their walks and talks, they began to share some of their personal stories. On one chilly March afternoon as they walked by the creek, Harriet learned that Reverend Harvey had earned his divinity degree at Boston University and, after graduating, had taken a Methodist church in Concord, an upscale suburb of Boston. He had married his sister's closest friend, and they had two daughters, now grown, one living in Boston and the other on the West coast. After his wife was killed in an automobile accident two years ago, he'd felt the need for a change and had found his way to Cottonwood Creek.

"How is it for you here?" Harriet asked him. "I imagine it's a different kind of congregation than you had in Concord."

Reverend Harvey smiled. "Indeed it is. Southeastern Colorado has its own unique culture. But I like it. There are good people in this town, and they've been warm and welcoming."

They walked awhile in silence. Two red-winged blackbirds, newly arrived, chirped to each other in the reeds at the creek's edge.

"I'm lonely, though," Reverend Harvey confessed. "I'm still not used to living by myself, and there's always a distance between a pastor and his congregation." He turned to her with a smile. "For some reason I don't feel that distance with you. I really enjoy your visits."

They walked farther. Harriet felt herself blushing, touched and honored by what he'd said.

"The manse is too big for one person and kind of shabby," he said after a while. "I don't know quite how to fix it up. But it's okay for now."

I could help him, Harriet thought, but she didn't dare offer.

Another day, it was rainy, and they had tea in the manse and spoke of their marriages.

"What was your wife like?" Harriet asked.

Reverend Harvey tilted his head, smiling as he remembered. "She was warm and playful, a great mom, devoted to our daughters, and very active in the church. A true helpmate, as the saying goes." He paused, held his breath for a moment, then released a quiet sigh. "I still miss her."

Harriet reached over to touch his hand.

He gestured to the tea pot. "More tea?"

"Yes, thank you."

Reverend Harvey refilled her cup and handed it to her.

"You haven't spoken of your marriage," he said. "I've heard you were recently divorced. How are you doing with that?"

"Okay now." Harriet sipped her tea. "It was tough at first, of course. He just threw me out, but I'm much better off without him. It was never a good marriage. We had fun together at the beginning, but then he became successful—he was a lawyer—and obsessed with his image. When I started limping and using a cane, I didn't fit that image. So he moved on to someone younger."

Reverend Harvey frowned. "Did you have any children?"

"No. That was the hardest part. I wanted children more than anything. Even at the beginning I had doubts about him, but I … well, I didn't think I'd have another chance, so I married him because I wanted a family. But he didn't want one. He kept putting it off and finally said absolutely no. I should have left him then … I never really loved him."

Harriet put her cup down and looked up at Reverend Harvey. "I *have* known love. I know what it's like to really love someone. I never felt that way about Jared."

Reverend Harvey tilted his head, question in his eyes. Harriet tensed all over; her stomach roiled in panic. What was she saying? She was so comfortable with Reverend Harvey she'd almost spilled her secret.

"What happened with the one you loved?" he asked.

Harriet couldn't breathe. Her heart pounded in her chest. "It was impossible," was all she could say.

Reverend Harvey gazed at her, his keen eyes penetrating her grief.

"Tell me about your daughters," Harriet said hastily.

He seemed glad to do that, and the conversation moved to safer territory.

❧ ☙

Every time they met, Reverend Harvey wanted to know about her communication with the bubbles, as they called them, and what was happening in her healing work. Except for Brenda, he was the only person she could talk with about such things, and he had a deeper perspective than Brenda's practical approach. She shared with him her confusion when the Song bounced back, the words and messages she had received, her grief that she could not help all those who crowded outside her door. And he listened in a way that helped her express her feelings more clearly. Sometimes they talked about God, a concept that was vague and uncomfortable for Harriet.

"But don't you see?" he asked her one afternoon as they sat on rocks at the creek's edge. "It's the *words* about God that trouble you, not God Himself. You live every day in His love. As we all do. But for you with the Song … You are exceptionally blessed because you *experience* God's love so strongly every day, every time the Song heals someone you touch."

"It's true," Harriet was quiet, her eyes closed, her face tilted up, reliving the power and glory of the Song healing through her. She opened her eyes and turned to him. "It's true. I do live in the experience of love when the Song is moving through me. Maybe it's from God, but it seems to come through the Song and the angels, if there are angels, or the bubbles, whatever they are. I just don't know what to believe."

"The belief doesn't really matter," he said. "It's only words. It's the compassion and caring you give that matters."

Harriet thought that was an odd thing for a minister to say, but found it comforting.

Spring

Spring unfolded unevenly, with increasing warm days and short late frosts, as was the way of Rocky Mountain springtime.

Finally, by mid-May the threat of frost was over. Harriet planted two rose bushes, one white and one pink, on either side of her front door. The seedlings she'd nurtured on her window sill were already blooming, and she set them out along her front walk—deep blue lobelia, white and lavender alyssum, and pink, purple, and white petunias. On her back patio she planted tomatoes, basil, and greens in box planters. She loved getting her hands in the earth, drinking in the rich, loamy smell of it, and bringing her little garden to life. Sometimes Tiger would leap onto the high fence that separated her patio from Leah's and jump down to keep her company.

One warm, soft afternoon in late May, she knelt on the grass weeding the flowers along her front walk. She paused, sat back on her heels, looked up into the new leaves unfolding on the trees, and was suddenly swept with the sweet urgency of springtime. Life force surged up in her in a way it hadn't for years. Her breasts tingled. She wrapped her arms around her chest. A memory arose from that long-ago summer with Neal. She was lying in his arms in post-sex bliss and he was stroking her breasts.

"I'm afraid they're not very big," Harriet had apologized.

"They're perfect," Neal had said, "small but well-shaped. And your nipples are like pink rosebuds." He turned on his side and drew one into his mouth, flicking it with his tongue until she thought she would die of the sweetness of it. For the first time, she was glad she had been born a girl. And strangely, after that her breasts did grow a little, as if they only needed affirmation to come into their fullness.

As she remembered, Harriet squeezed her arms tighter across her chest and rocked from side to side. I'm past menopause, she thought, but not past longing to be loved.

On weekends, Harriet began taking long walks, high into the hills, cherishing the alone time to muse after her busy work week. Because healing with the Song had such dramatic effect, issues that Harriet had often wondered about over the years of her practice now stood out in sharper relief.

How much of healing was the responsibility of the patient? Karl, the obese man with the painful knees, had come to her recently, having gotten in on a cancellation. The Song had restored the cartilage in his damaged knees, but Harriet knew that carrying around his three hundred plus pounds would soon wear them down again. She told Karl that, referred him to a dietitian to help him with a diet, but she could tell from the look on his face that he had no intention of dieting. He would just come back to her when they started to hurt again.

Harriet remembered Eliza Riley's outburst when she told Harriet she was closing her practice in Denver: "I've had it. All day long they come in, lie on the table, 'Fix me, fix me,' and never take responsibility for themselves.

"I straighten out Josie's back three times a week. She wears five-inch spike heels and skirts so skinny they tie her legs together down to her knees. How a human woman can take a step dressed like that, I can't imagine. 'Come down to earth,' I tell her. 'Get some flat shoes and a skirt wide enough to walk in.' But no. Image is more important than comfort. I wonder if she'll change her ways when I'm not here to put her back together.

"Then there's Mike the muscle man, so bent on bulging that he keeps going to the gym doing the same thing over and over that messes up his low back. I say, 'Cool the crunches,' but he's back again in a week. He's got to have his six-pack abs, never mind that they pull his sternum down into his pubes and compress his lumbars. Surprise. He's in pain again, but never mind, Dr. Reilly will fix it."

She pushed a lock of dark hair back off her brow, her blue eyes flashing.

"Of course, it's because they keep coming back that your business thrives," Harriet had suggested.

"True, true. But I have this feeling of futility. Also I'm tired of the city. I'm going back to New England, find a cabin by a lake, and write novels. That may also be futile, but at least I'll enjoy myself."

Harriet chuckled, remembering. Eliza had always had a way about her.

There was also the issue of underlying causes. After finding the second tumor in her mother's lung and talking with Reverend Harvey, Harriet become intrigued with seeking the issues underlying the symptoms the Song healed so readily. She had known for years that there were layers to healing, but when the Song first came to her and the symptoms disappeared so quickly, she had forgotten to attend to the deeper layers. Now that was her focus, and she found she could guide the Song to seek those layers—often ones of trauma and emotional wounding. Her work had become exciting to her in new ways.

⁊ ⁋

Every day there would be moments, whether she was touching her patients, or kneeling in her garden, or hiking in the hills, when she felt such gratitude for her wellbeing, that she would whisper a prayer of thanks to the unseen beings who had healed her and given her the Song so she could heal others.

She felt blessed beyond understanding. Not only was the sciatic pain gone, but she felt stronger, more alive than she'd ever felt in her life. And her practice continued to be a wonder as she lived her days in the ecstasy of the trance, still in awe each time of the miracles that unfolded under her hands.

One early morning, she climbed to the top of the ridge and sat watching the sun sparkle on the lake below her. The new grass was soft and green, coming up between the brown blades of last year's grass. Her body felt warm and alive, and she was washed anew with the joy of wellbeing. Then she did something she hadn't done before. She began to *sing* her prayer of gratitude. They answered, a wordless song, yet she understood that they heard and rejoiced that she was singing to them as they sang to her. For a long time they sang together, and Harriet felt an even deeper connection than she had felt before, a depth of love and oneness that erased her boundaries.

A week later, on a Saturday afternoon after a long, steep hike, as she lay in a high meadow under peaceful ponderosas, it all came together for her.

I'm communicating with them telepathically, she realized. That's how they communicate with me. The Song doesn't have words. It never did, unless I pour it through a hymn or some other song. When they sing to me I don't even hear it with my ears, but inside. When I sing to them, or they sing to me, meaning comes through.

She sat straight up. Then maybe I can ask them about underlying causes. How do I do it?

She sat still, waiting. The wind sighed through the ponderosas. She spoke the word *eliria* and immediately felt a response, a tingling, a thread of melody.

I know, she thought. I'll hold the question and then start singing and maybe the Song will carry my question to them.

She shaped her question in her mind. *I can see how the Song heals the symptoms, but I don't know how it affects the underlying causes. Please tell me about that.*

Then she sang, letting the Song pour through her, reaching out with her love.

She sang until she sensed she had been heard, then waited.

Their response had a questioning quality. Several voices wove as if they were asking each other her question, like the time she had asked why her mother's tumor came back.

The Song shifted. One voice, rich and full, sang, *We don't understand underlying causes.*

Harriet's heart sank. *You can heal anything. Why don't you understand?* she sang.

The same rich, resonant voice answered, *We are only learning about humans, about pain. On Eliria there is no pain.*

Harriet was so startled by this message that she lost the connection. *Wait!* she called. But with a soft *Ah*, the voices drifted away. One word remained. *Kiria.*

Harriet walked slowly down the trail, trying to make sense of the strange communication.

It sounds like eliria is a place. But I've never heard of it. It's not in the dictionary. Where on earth could it be?

I've never heard of a place where people communicate telepathically.

Never of a place where there is no pain.

It can't be a real place.

What do they mean they are only learning about humans? That doesn't make sense. How could they heal me so perfectly if they don't understand humans?

Who *are* they? That's what I should have asked them.

Chapter 19

Compassionate Care Nursing Home

The next afternoon, Harriet pulled into the parking lot of the Compassionate Care Nursing Home. She didn't get out right away but sat staring at the large building in front of her with its gardens full of early summer flowers, seeking to calm the tension in her belly. She hoped what she was about to do would be okay.

A few weeks before, one of her patients, a young woman named Susan who volunteered at Compassionate Care, had asked her to sing for the residents. They had a Sunday afternoon program, Susan explained. Harriet had such a lovely voice when she healed. Could she also use it to sing some songs, maybe some hymns?

Harriet had made the mistake of telling Susan about singing in the church in her home town. Then there was no escape.

So here she was, sitting in the parking lot, full of trepidation. It should be fine, she told herself. Like singing in church. Susan was a pianist. They'd practiced together the day before and she'd sung only hymns. No weird words, no overtones. It should be fine.

She gathered up her music and opened the car door.

Susan met her in the entry way and guided her to a large meeting room with windows looking out over a lawn and several trees. Some of the residents were already sitting in rows of chairs facing an open area with the piano to one side. Others were coming in slowly, leaning on canes and walkers, pushed in wheelchairs. Harriet felt a lump come into her throat as she observed the bent bodies, the pale faces, and dim eyes.

When everyone was settled, Susan introduced Harriet, then sat down at the piano and played the opening bars of "Have Thine Own Way, Lord." As Harriet began to sing, the Song and the love poured through the hymn, and the trance descended. The room remained hushed as Harriet sang hymn after hymn. Harriet saw tears running down wrinkled cheeks. She sang for almost an hour, ending with her two favorite arias from *The Messiah*: "He Shall Feed His Flock" and "Come Unto Him."

When the last notes of the piano ended, Harriet came back to herself. Her first thought was to make a quick getaway before those old people had time to get to their feet or get their wheelchairs rolling. She stepped quickly to the piano to gather up her music, but she had not reckoned on Susan, who jumped up and threw her arms around Harriet.

"You sounded beautiful when we practiced yesterday, but this was totally different. It was like when you healed me, but you were only singing hymns, not that other language. What happened?"

Harriet loosened Susan's arms. "The healing Song comes through when I'm with people who need it," she said softly, not wanting others to hear. People were stirring now, but the room was still quiet.

"Did you heal all of them?"

"No, I need to touch for that to happen." Out of the corner of her eye, Harriet saw the old people approaching. "I need to go now."

But it was too late. They gathered around her, blessing her, thanking her, reaching out to touch her. With each touch Harriet felt the Song stir in her. She became anxious.

Then a tall, thin woman hurrying toward her, leaning on her cane, caught her foot on the leg of a chair and fell with a crash. Everyone in the room turned. A low groan of empathy moved like a wave through the crowd. The woman lay still, then rolled and cried out. Several attendants rushed to her side.

"My arm," the woman moaned.

"Oh, Lydia," one the attendants said. "Please, not another broken bone."

Harriet wavered. With all the attention turned toward the woman on the floor, she could escape. Instead, she found herself kneeling on the floor, laying her hand on Lydia's back.

One of the attendants rushed out to call a doctor. Several others moved through the crowd, assisting the elderly residents to move back.

Susan knelt beside Harriet. "Sing to her. You can make it well. She's only just recovering from a broken hip. It's too awful that she fell again."

Harriet looked up at the attendant kneeling on the other side of Lydia. "Would it be all right if I sing to her while we wait for the doctor?"

"Oh, yes," the attendant said. "Please."

Harriet released the Song in all its power and strangeness. Immediately she saw how fragile all the bones were, the break in the upper arm, the barely healed hip. She also saw weakened kidneys, a clogged heart. Moving her hands gently over the broken arm, she watched the Song knit the bones together, then laying her hand on Lydia's chest, she saw all the other bones strengthened, the kidneys renewed, the heart cleared.

The Song subsided. Harriet lifted her hands and settled back on her heels.

Lydia sat up. She moved her arm, held it out in front of her. "It doesn't hurt!" she exclaimed in wonder. She looked at Harriet, her eyes wide. "It doesn't hurt," she repeated. She unwound her long legs and stood, ignoring the cane that still lay where she had fallen. She took a few tentative steps, then strode out across the room. The crowd parted to let her pass. "I can walk!" she cried. "Look at me. I can walk without my cane!"

A bent old man rolled his wheelchair up to Harriet. "Sing for me, too," he begged. "I want to walk again."

Still kneeling on the floor, Harriet looked up into his faded, watery eyes. The Song was rising in her, pressing her from the inside. Behind the man in the wheelchair were thirty or more people, all focused on her with longing in their faces. Harriet felt as if she stood on a precipice. Glimpsing the consequences of what she was about to do, she wavered. Only for a moment.

She got up off the floor and laid her hands on the shoulders of the man in the wheelchair. The Song burst forth. All afternoon, she sang and touched. The Song barely paused as she moved from one to the next. All around her those who had been healed were laughing, weeping, hugging each other, walking, jumping, skipping—wheelchairs, canes, and walkers discarded. Those not yet healed pressed close. Still lost in the trance, Harriet sang, turning to the next person who waited with hope in her eyes, until everyone in the room had been healed.

As the celebration swirled around her, Harriet stood, arms loose at her sides, limp with awe. Across the room she saw a man with a black bag in his hand come through the door and stop at the sight before him.

The doctor?

Lydia took her hand. "Olivia was too sick to come. She's bad off. Come with me to her room and sing for her." Harriet turned quickly, before the man's searching eyes could find her. She followed Lydia down a long corridor to a room where a woman lay connected to oxygen and an IV. She was pale and still under the sheet.

Standing in the doorway, Harriet saw that Olivia was clearly near death. She could smell it in the room.

Lydia said, excitedly, "Olivia, this is Harriet. If she sings to you, you'll be well again, healed of everything wrong. She healed everyone who came to her concert this afternoon. Look at me. I'm walking without my cane."

"Hush," Harriet said, holding up her hand. Lydia drew back. Harriet went to Olivia's bedside.

Olivia turned her head toward Harriet. Their eyes met. "No," she said, her voice husky, barely audible. "No singing. Let me go."

Even as her eyes still met Harriet's, her gaze receded, taking her consciousness back into herself. She turned her head away.

Harriet's throat ached. Gently she touched Olivia's hand. The Song did not arise. "Blessings on your journey," she said softly.

⁓ ⁓

Harriet sat at the little table on her patio, her half-eaten supper forgotten on her plate. She leaned her head in her hand.

The memory of Olivia's husky voice saying "Let me go," and the image of her receding gaze were still vivid in Harriet's mind. Juxtaposed with that image was another—the big room full of moving, rejoicing old people. And the man who was probably the doctor standing by the door, watching.

What have I done? Harriet asked herself. What if all those old people, like Olivia, were also preparing to die, but had been caught up in the excitement of the moment? She knew the healings had cured all that was amiss in each person. Even though they still had white hair and wrinkled faces, they were completely healthy. How long would they live now? Did they *want* to continue to live a long time?

Would the healing last? She remembered the tumor that had come back in her mother's lung. What if they left the nursing home feeling fine and then all their difficulties came back?

She sighed and rubbed her brow. I don't know what I'm doing, she thought. Maybe I've made a terrible mistake.

And, of course, they would tell people. Just when Brenda had finally established some order in the practice.

What had come over her that she had acted so impulsively, abandoned all caution?

She knew. The memory of her own pain and limitation was still fresh. She would have traveled to the other side of the world to find someone who could heal her as she could heal with the Song. There had been so many times in her practice when she had been unable to resolve the distress of her patients and had longed for such a gift as she now had.

How could she have turned away?

She knew. The memory of her own pain and limitation was still
Harriet hurried into her office the next morning, just as her first client arrived. She'd had a restless night and then overslept. She was weary, but soon dropped into the trance of the Song, her cares falling into the background.

She had a full schedule and didn't connect with Brenda, except in passing, until lunch time. On the edge of her consciousness, she was aware of the phone ringing often.

When they sat down to lunch together, Brenda looked grim. "What in the world did you do yesterday?" she asked Harriet.

Harriet tensed. "I sang at Compassionate Care. You knew I was going to do that."

"You were just going to sing hymns."

"Yes. I started that way. Then it sort of got out of hand."

"I'll say. Honey, you've stirred up a storm."

Here it comes, Harriet thought. "Uh-oh. What?"

"I got a call from the head nurse, who's also the manager over there. Mrs. Maloney her name is. She said you unloosed chaos. She wants to talk with you. Right away, she says. I told her you had a full day. Then she wants to know when you'll be done and insists you come over then. I told her I'd speak to you and get back to her. What do you want me to tell her?"

"Oh, my." Harriet felt her stomach tighten. "I guess I'd better go. Tell her I'll come at five fifteen. Will she still be there then?"

"She said she'd be there until six."

"Oh, no."

"Honey, what did you do? It sounds like you gave them more than a sweet concert."

"I did rather." Harriet sucked in her breath between her teeth, then went on to describe what she now began to think of as a healing binge, ending with the story of the woman who didn't want to be healed. "What kind of chaos?"

"Oh, my God. Listen, honey. What do you think those old folks are gonna do now that they're all well? They won't want to hang out in a nursing home. They're all gonna be peeling out of there, leaving empty beds and taking their money with them."

"I didn't think of that, the money part. But they were happy—running around, laughing and crying. I slipped out the back way after I visited Olivia. You know how I am."

"For a woman who doesn't want to be noticed, you've sure got yourself in a pickle. Mrs. Maloney isn't the half of it. The phone's been ringing off the hook. The word is out and there's reporters wanting to talk to you, a bunch of 'em. And the doctor from the nursing home. Some of the reporters are hanging around outside, listening to you sing. I had to lock the door and hold 'em back when I let your patients in. You're gonna need to use the back window this afternoon."

❧ ❧

The parking lot of Compassionate Care was busy when Harriet arrived. One of the women she'd touched the afternoon before was sitting in the front seat of a car, while a middle-aged couple loaded suitcases into the back. When she saw Harriet, she flung the car door open and ran to embrace her.

"Thank you, thank you!" she exclaimed. "I feel so wonderful. I'm going home. This is my daughter and her husband."

The daughter and her husband looked harried. Harriet acknowledged the introductions hastily. She was late for her appointment with Mrs. Maloney.

In the curved driveway outside the main entrance, another car was being loaded. Inside, the halls were bustling with people moving in and out of the rooms carrying boxes and suitcases. A small, bald man swinging a duffel bag headed for the door, chanting, "I'm outta here. I'm outta here." Harriet remembered him well. Harold. The Song had showed her the withered part of his brain, the plaques and scrambled circuitry, and she had watched in wonder as all was renewed.

Someone called, "The healer is here!" More doors flew open, and Harriet was surrounded by those the Song had healed and their relatives who had come to take them home.

A young attendant pushed through to her. "Mrs. Maloney is waiting," she said. "Let's go this way." She led Harriet down a side corridor, away from the bustle. "Mrs. Maloney's kind of upset," she said. "But don't pay any attention to what she says. She wasn't there. She didn't see what happened." The young woman looked up at Harriet with tears in her eyes. "I'll never forget it. It was the most awesome thing I've ever experienced. I never heard anything so beautiful as your singing."

She stopped outside a closed door and knocked.

Mrs. Maloney was square-shouldered and stocky. Her short, permed hair was iron gray, as were her eyes, and there were deep, downward lines at the sides of her mouth.

She dismissed the attendant and gestured to a chair. Harriet sat down, struggling to keep her head up, feeling like a small child in the principal's office. All the words she'd prepared on the way over fled from her mind.

"I suppose you saw as you came in," Mrs. Maloney said. "Everything is in an uproar here. Because of what you did yesterday. You were invited only to give a concert. What were you thinking?"

Harriet drew in her breath. "I didn't plan it," she managed finally. "I did give a concert and was ready to leave when Lydia fell. They told me she was just recovering from a broken hip … I couldn't turn away."

"What exactly did you do?"

"I sang."

"You sang. So I heard. Explain yourself."

Harriet hesitated. Anything but some portion of the truth would probably get her in more hot water. She took another deep breath. "Several months ago, I had a near-death experience, and when I came back I found that, if there were need, I could see into a body that I touched and the Song that came through me would heal whatever was amiss. So I let the Song through to heal Lydia's broken arm and other difficulties she had. Then everyone wanted me to sing for them. So I did."

Mrs. Maloney folded her arms across the shelf of her bosom and riveted Harriet with a long, silent stare. So long that Harriet's heart began to flutter.

Finally Mrs. Maloney spoke. "I don't know what to make of such a story. But clearly, whatever the cause, you were effective. Not only are they all up and walking, but I've had the vitals checked on everyone you touched. All the vitals are perfect. Do you realize I could have you arrested for practicing medicine without a license?"

"No," Harriet said firmly. "You could not. I was not practicing medicine—no drugs, no surgery. I was simply singing. And I do have a license. I am a licensed chiropractor in good standing."

"I know that. I've done some research on you today. You're the one they wrote up in the paper last January for healing that boy, Jack. But being a chiropractor doesn't license you to repair broken bones. I almost did call the police, but I thought I'd see what you had to say for yourself first."

She glared at Harriet. "Do you realize what you've done? You've turned those people's lives upside down. Most of them came here to die. They'd given up their homes and most of their possessions. Where will they go? Harold Beaner came to say good-bye and when I asked him, he said he had no plans; he was just leaving. He had severe Alzheimer's. I don't know what will happen to him."

"I saw him as I came in," Harriet said.

"After you sang to him, he remembered a few things I wish he hadn't," Mrs. Maloney went on. "He stole a car yesterday evening. He used to work in a car lot and knew how to break into a locked car and hot wire it. He remembered all that just fine. Yesterday morning he couldn't remember his name. One of our nurses went to go home, and her car was gone. Oh, he brought it back okay, no harm done. But he also brought back a couple of cases of beer, and then all of them, nurses and attendants included, were larking it up in the dining room until late last night. The place was a mess when I came in this morning."

Harriet held the corners of her mouth firmly down, repressing an unruly rush of laughter.

As if she sensed Harriet's stifled mirth, Mrs. Maloney glared more fiercely. "You turned this place upside down. The folks who didn't come to your concert were upset by all the noise last night and are even more upset by everyone leaving today. You didn't get to all of them, you know."

"I know. Lydia took me to see Olivia, but she didn't want me to sing to her."

"She died this morning. In the midst of everything."

"Oh." Harriet felt her heart contract. "I knew she was near."

"You also need to know—" Mrs. Maloney's voice grew more severe. "All the families of those you fixed up are not delighted to have them well again. Mrs. Evans was dying, but they took her to hear your concert. Now she's fine, and her son and his family may lose their home. They came and talked to me this morning. They don't know what they are going to do, or what to do with her. They were behind on their mortgage and counting on the son's inheritance to bail them out."

Harriet bent her head, feeling uncertain, then indignant. Was a mortgage reason enough to withhold the easing of an old woman's suffering? She remembered the joy in the faces of those who had been healed. She lifted her head again and looked into Mrs. Maloney's face. "Don't you care about your patients? Aren't you glad they're well now and out of pain, able to move freely again, live a little longer?"

Mrs. Maloney jutted her chin out. "Of course I care. Why do you think I'm so concerned? Living longer. Where will they go? Some of them have families, but maybe those families don't want their elderly relative moving in. Mrs. Hendricks is as mean and bossy as they come. Her son didn't look at all happy when he came to pick her up. What if they don't have families? How are they going to support themselves? What are they going to do with their lives now that their lives aren't ending after all? You should know that some of those people who are leaving have signed a do-not-resuscitate order."

Harriet gasped inwardly. Maybe she really *had* made a terrible mistake. "They were very happy," she protested.

"Yes, of course. But after the excitement's over, what then?"

Harriet twisted in her chair. She felt exhausted and overwhelmed. It had been a long day. One of the reporters had seen her climbing out the back window, and she'd had to run for her car. She didn't know what she would do if they found out where she lived.

"I'm sorry to have caused you so much trouble," she said to Mrs. Maloney. "Is there anything you want me to do?"

Mrs. Maloney fixed her with another long stare. "No. There's nothing you can do now, but I want you to understand that when you upset the natural order of things, there are repercussions."

There was a knock on the door. Mrs. Maloney went to open it. After a brief exchange with the young attendant, she turned back to Harriet. "I need to go now. I won't call the police. But don't ever do such a thing again."

⌒⌒

Twenty minutes later, Harriet pulled into the parking place behind her condo. There was a back gate through to her patio, but she decided to go around front and water the flowers along the walk on her way in.

As she emerged from the path between the buildings, she saw a white car parked on the street in front of her home. Inside sat a man, watching her front door.

She stopped, frozen. She recognized that profile. It was the reporter with the hook nose and wire-rimmed glasses who had come to her office back in January.

Her first impulse was to turn and run. Dealing with him was the last thing she needed at that moment. Then fear morphed into anger. She was done with running. She stood firmly at the corner of her little front lawn, her jaw clenched.

He had seen her. He moved quickly out of his car and across the narrow strip of grass between the street and her front walk. He approached and held out his hand. "Dr. Ellis? I'm Joel Peterson from the Daily Camera. I'd like to have a few words with you."

Harriet stood stiff and silent. She did not take his hand.

Mr. Peterson did not seem daunted. "I need to talk with you," he said authoritatively. "I understand you did an amazing healing at the Compassionate Care Nursing Home, gave thirty or more old folks back their youth."

Harriet remained silent, her anger overcoming her inherent courtesy. "I have no comment," she said finally, and turned to go up her walk.

In three quick steps, Mr. Peterson placed himself between her and her front porch. "Now Dr. Ellis, this is an extraordinary event. You are clearly a gifted healer, and people want to know more about you. How did you accomplish the healings? We need the details."

Harriet cringed inside, her anger rising. The last thing she wanted was for people to know more about her. Her green eyes flashed. Her voice was ice. "I said I have no comment."

"I'd just like a few words. How did you come by your gift of healing? How long—?"

Harriet cut him off. "Mr. Peterson, I will not, I repeat, *will not*, discuss that or anything else with you." She took a step toward him. "Please move aside. I want to go in."

She could see he was wavering, but he was nothing if not persistent.

"Dr. Ellis, I will only take a moment of your time …"

She took another step toward him. He was tall, but she was taller. For the first time she was glad of her six feet.

He retreated and stumbled against the bottom step of her front porch.

"Leave now," Harriet ordered him. "You are trespassing and harassing me. Do I need to call the police?"

I sound like Mrs. Maloney, she thought wildly.

But it worked. "Yes. All right. Good evening, Dr. Ellis." Mr. Peterson did not quite run to his car.

The moment the way was clear, Harriet was on her front porch, right up against the green front door, digging in her bag for her keys. She unlocked the door, strode through, and slammed it behind her. In one long step she reached the cord by the front window. As she pulled the blind down, she caught a glimpse of the white car driving away.

Shaking all over, she dropped into the rocking chair in the dimmed living room. Her worst fear realized. They had found her home.

Gradually her shaking subsided. After a while, she got up and went into her bedroom. The window looked out onto her patio and the evening sky, soft with the pink glow of sunset.

I need to go out, she thought. Walk. I want to go to the lake. She found herself trembling again. Will they find me even there?

"Damn!" she said aloud, spinning away from the window. "I'm not going to hide in my house." She remembered Sophie telling her she shouldn't walk alone at night. "It isn't night yet," she said, as if answering Sophie. Swiftly she changed into shorts, tee shirt, and sandals.

Her adrenaline was still high when she reached the lake. At first she walked fast, her long strides taking her rapidly around the first arc of the path, but gradually she slowed as the beauty of early summer twilight, cloud reflections in the water, the song of a meadowlark eased her spirit.

As dusk turned to darkness, she returned home, fixed herself a simple meal, took a long hot bath, and went to bed. But sleep eluded her. All her doubts and fears arose again, and she lay awake until the wee hours of the morning.

Chapter 20

Death in the Family

She was waked before six by the phone ringing. Half conscious, she tensed. The reporters? Her phone was a land line, unlisted. Surely Brenda wouldn't have given out the number.

The phone kept ringing, jabbing her awake. She rolled on her side and looked at the screen. It was Sophie.

"Harrie?" Sophie was crying.

"I'm here. Sophie, what's wrong?"

"Dad died last night. All of a sudden." Sophie's words came out in a rush, broken by sobs. Their father had had a stroke. Their mother had waked and found him struggling in the bed beside her, unable to speak. She'd called an ambulance.

"But you know," Sophie sobbed, "how long it takes an ambulance to get to our hick town all the way from Parker. By the time it arrived, Dad was dead. I was at Mom's house by then, and he was dead. Not breathing. No heartbeat. But still they tried to resuscitate him … in the ambulance … all the way to the hospital. Mom and I rode with them. It was awful. They just kept pumping on him."

"Oh, Sophie."

"Mom wouldn't believe Dad was dead until we got to the hospital and the doctor told her. Then she just shrank. She's sitting in the waiting room, all collapsed in a chair, not saying anything. Can you come? We need you."

Harriet's mind spun. Dad dead? She could hear Sophie crying against her ear and, outside the open window, early morning bird song.

She caught in a quick breath. "Of course I'll come. Where will you be? Parker? Home?"

"I don't know. Jim is here; he followed the ambulance in his car. He called Meyers Funeral Home, but they're not open yet. Then they'll have to come all the way up here to get Dad. We have to wait here until they come. I don't know where we'll be."

Sophie sounded lost, unlike her usual competent self. Harriet was glad her husband was with her.

"I'll leave as soon as I can," she said. "I'll bring my cell phone and call when I get close. Tell Mom I'm coming."

❧ ☙

She was on the road in less than an hour. She'd called Brenda and asked her to close the office and cancel the rest of the week, knowing her family would need her at least that long. The morning traffic in Denver required all her attention, but once the city was behind her, she was able to let go into her thoughts and feelings.

Dad dead. Images of him flashed through her mind—holding little Sophie in his lap, tilting his head back as he laughed, frowning with disapproval, greeting customers in the shoe store, more recently sitting in his chair by the stove, a drink in his hand. She'd never been close to him as Sophie had been. Her failure to be a boy had always impeded their relationship. Nothing she had ever done had earned his love. And now it was too late. At least she didn't have to try anymore. With that thought, she sighed with relief. Then winced in guilt.

She drove on, her fingers tight around the wheel. In spite of her difficulty with her dad, he and her mother and the house she'd grown up in had been her foundation. What would happen now? What would her mother do without Dad who had been the center of her life since she married him at age seventeen?

Maybe once she gets over the shock, Harriet thought, she'll be better off without his constant demands and criticism.

Then she started thinking about the nursing home adventure and Mrs. Maloney's lecture. Nausea stirred in her stomach. What *will* become of all those old people the Song had healed only two days ago?

Harriet hunched her shoulders. And the reporters— Oh, Harriet realized. Her dad's death had given her good reason to disappear. She imagined the papers saying, "Dr. Ellis could not be reached for comment." Maybe by the time she got home again, it would have all blown over. She hoped.

She stopped in the next small town for gas and a quick breakfast. While she was waiting for her food, she pulled out her cell phone and called Sophie. Sophie was calmer. The folks from Meyers Funeral Home had come and taken their father back to Cottonwood Creek, and Jim was driving her and their mother home.

An hour later, Harriet pulled up in front of her childhood home. Jim's car was in the driveway. Harriet hurried into the house and folded her mother in her arms.

Later that day, Sophie and Harriet sat at the kitchen table with their mother.

"Have you made arrangements?" Sophie asked. "Several years ago I gave you a batch of papers from Meyer's about reserving a burial plot and the kind of funeral you wanted and all. Remember? I didn't know then Dad was going to die so soon, but I thought, at your age, you should get that set up. Did you ever fill those out?"

Their mother shook her head. "No. I never did. I forgot all about it. Harry kept me so busy looking after his every little need, I just forgot. I don't even know where those papers are." She fluttered her hands.

Sophie captured her mother's hand. "It's okay, Mom. We can handle it now."

"The funeral ..." Tears came to their mother's eyes. "Reverend Harvey's been over and asked ... when I wanted to do it and how and all ... I have no idea ..."

Harriet had been running some errands for her mother when Reverend Harvey stopped by that morning.

She took her mother's other hand. "Would you like me to talk with Reverend Harvey, make some plans that you can look over?"

"Oh, honey. Please. That would help so much. I just don't know ..."

"I'll take care of it, Mom."

❧ ❧

Harriet stood, hesitant, in the open door of Reverend Harvey's office.

He looked up and saw her. "Harriet. Come in. I was so sorry to hear of your dad's death. And sorry to have missed you yesterday when I stopped by."

Still standing in the doorway, Harriet blurted. "I need your help. I have to plan the funeral. Mom can't deal with it. She just falls apart at the thought. I told her I'd handle it, but I don't know how either."

Reverend Harvey came to her and took both her hands in his. "Of course I'll help you. It's my job. I'll be doing the service. Come, sit down." He pulled out a chair and sat facing her, taking her hands in his again. "I've been thinking of you and your family, thinking of the service. We'll create something beautiful for your dad."

Harriet slumped with relief. Ever since Sophie's call the morning before, she'd been focused on being the strong one, taking care of her mother and sister. Now Reverend Harvey was there with his kind eyes, his warm hands holding hers. He'd know what to do. He'd done lots of funerals.

With the relief, all the grief and confusion she'd been holding back welled up in her. She found she was shaking.

"How are you doing?" he asked. His voice was gentle, his eyes warm with compassion.

"Mostly okay." She caught her breath. "It was a shock. He wouldn't let me help him. He sent the Song bouncing back every time I tried, but I'd seen inside, so I knew … Still, when it actually happens … nothing prepares you."

Harriet gripped Reverend Harvey's hands tighter, trying to stop the shaking.

"So I knew he couldn't last much longer. I didn't say anything to Mom and Sophie, so it was more of a shock for them."

"What about your other sister—Emma, is it?"

"We've called her. Her phone has a message saying she's on retreat and can't be reached until Friday. After being arrow-straight all her life, she's gotten involved with some weird, New Age spiritual teacher. We left a message. Mom really wants her to be here for the funeral."

"So we shouldn't do it before Saturday."

"Saturday was when I was thinking."

Reverend Harvey moved to his desk and picked up a pad and pencil. "Let's make a plan." For the next hour they planned the service. As they worked, Harriet's shaking eased. They chose hymns and Scripture that Harriet's mother liked and set the time for two in the afternoon.

"What about flowers?" Harriet asked. "Are there other details we need to handle?"

"Many more details, like what kind of casket, if you want a viewing at the funeral home, whether to have an open or closed casket at the service. And you'll need to pick out a site in the graveyard."

"Oh, no." Harriet paled.

He set down his pad and looked across the desk at her. "Don't worry, Harriet. I'm here. I'll be right with you for the whole process. The folks at the funeral home can advise us, and, once they know what you want, they'll take care of it all. Why don't we walk over there now. It's just around the corner."

He took her arm and led her out of the church. The summer afternoon was warm. There was a fresh breeze off the creek, and the streets were quiet, only an occasional car passing. A woman working in the flower bed in front of her house called out a greeting.

Harriet returned the woman's greeting. It's so peaceful and friendly here, she thought.

Harriet and Reverend Harvey spent another hour at the funeral home. Mr. Meyers himself helped them. They chose a simple wooden casket and planned a viewing for Friday afternoon and a closed casket for the church service. When all was settled, Mr. Meyer drove them out to the graveyard to choose a burial site.

The graveyard was at the north boundary of the town, spread over a low hill above the creek. Harriet chose a spot at the western edge near a cluster of old juniper trees.

"I can walk home from here," she told Mr. Meyer. "Thank you for your help."

"I'll walk with you," Reverend Harvey said.

Her original thought was that she wanted to have some time alone, to let all the events of the day settle. But she found as they set out, that she was glad of his presence beside her. He understood her mood without being told, and they walked in silence.

When they reached her house, he said, "I'll come by tomorrow and we can go over everything with your mother."

Harriet felt a rush of gratitude. "Reverend Harvey, how can I thank you? I now feel that getting through the next few days will be possible."

"That's what I'm here for," he said. He hesitated. "Harriet ... we don't need to be so formal. Why don't you call me Winston?"

His cheeks flushed, and Harriet caught another glimpse of his shy self. She felt a little awkward herself, but also touched.

"Okay," she said, smiling at him. "Thanks for seeing me home, Winston."

Harriet and Sophie sat with their mother in the living room, discussing her future. Harry Ellis's shabby, empty chair by the stove was a presence in the room, all its stains and worn places revealed in the morning sunlight.

"I think you should come to the ranch and live with us," Sophie said. "We have lots of space now, with all the kids gone except Albert. The room that used to be Mary's is pretty with lots of south light and the bathroom right next to it."

"No," their mother said firmly. "I want to stay right here in my home. I don't want to be way out there. I'd never see any of my friends. And how would I get to the quilting circle?"

Their mother had never learned to drive.

"But how will you manage all by yourself?" Sophie asked.

"Same as I've always managed," their mother answered. "I can walk to the store and to church like I've been doing. Jimmy brings over a check every month from the shoe store, and helps with the yard and snow shoveling. Harry hasn't done anything around here for years. I'll be fine."

Harriet sat quietly, listening. Something had shifted in her mother in the last twenty-four hours. A clarity and firmness that Harriet remembered from her childhood had reemerged. Suddenly Harriet was seeing not just her mother, but the woman, Amy Ellis, who had been a pillar of the church, kept the books for the shoe store, managed the household, and brought up her three girls kindly, but strictly. Harriet couldn't remember when it was that her mother had started becoming fluttery and unsure of herself.

"But won't you be lonely?" Sophie asked. "Without Dad?"

"He wasn't much company," her mother said, "except for fussing at me all the time to get him this and that. I'll be okay once I get through the funeral. And we have to do something with all his stuff."

"Sophie and I can help with that," Harriet said.

"I want that chair gone," her mother said emphatically, gesturing at the worn chair by the stove. It's a disgrace. I tried for years to get him a new one, but he wouldn't have it."

"You're going to get rid of Dad's chair?" Sophie asked. The tone of her voice suggested such action would be sacrilege.

"You can have it if you want."

Sophie looked over at Harriet. Harriet shrugged.

"And his clothes," their mother continued. "I'm thinking Jim and your boys and Mary's Bob can come take what they want and we'll put the rest in the donation box at church.

"I'll handle the clothes," Sophie said. "We can take care of the rest of his stuff little by little."

⁂

The next few days were a disorienting blur for Harriet. The doorbell rang frequently as the women of the quilting circle, friends and neighbors from all over town came bringing flowers, condolences, and food. The refrigerator was soon packed.

Harriet's main focus was to care for her mother and guide her through all the steps that had to be taken before the funeral. Her mother alternated between being clear and directive one moment and falling apart the next. At times she seemed angry as she ordered the rearrangement of the living room furniture, the removal of the chair, and the clearing out of her husband's closet.

Anger, Harriet mused. I can't remember her ever expressing anger, ever. Even this is subdued, but the energy is clear. Maybe that was behind the tumors. He never was considerate of her.

Emma arrived Friday noon, and that afternoon the three sisters and their mother sat in the funeral home receiving friends and neighbors who came to bid their farewells to Harry Ellis. Lots of people came. At one time or another, everyone in town had bought shoes at Harry's store.

Then it was Saturday—the service in the church, the procession following the black hearse through town to the graveyard, the burial. When the first shovelful of earth fell on the casket, Harriet felt her stomach sink and her knees go weak. Her father was really gone. Still she managed to stand strong between Sophie and her mother, her arms around them as they wept. Emma, dry-eyed like Harriet, supported their mother from the other side. All the family was gathered around them.

After the burial, the women of the quilting circle hosted a reception at the church.

One of the women came up to Harriet. "You didn't sing in the service."

"No … I couldn't."

"No wonder, poor dear." The woman patted Harriet's arm. "Are you going to sing tomorrow in church?"

"Not this time," Harriet answered. Underneath all the emotion around her father's death, she was still shaken by what had happened at the nursing home. She didn't know what the Song might do in the present circumstances and felt too fragile to risk it.

Then Neal's daughter, Nan, approached her. "I'm so sorry about your dad," she said. She bit her lip and tears came into her eyes. "I'm about to lose mine, too."

Harriet's breath stopped. "Oh, is it that bad?"

"Yes. He's home now." Nan pulled a tissue out of her pocket and wiped her eyes. "The folks at the treatment center said there was nothing more they could do for him, except pain relief. They gave him only a few weeks. So he decided to come home to die. I've hired a hospice nurse to take care of him full time. Roger and I go over every day and sit with him. He seems peaceful, just wants to be quiet."

Harriet struggled to hold back her tears.

"But he did ask me," Nan said. "When I told him Harry had died, he asked if you would be coming down for the funeral. I said I was sure you would. He asked if you would come visit him. He wants to see you before he dies. I know you have a lot to do with your family and all, but can you come? It seems important to him."

Harriet's heart raced, her eyes blurred. He wants to see *me*? Before he dies?

"Yes, of course, I can," she answered. "I need to be with my family this evening. Could I come tomorrow afternoon?"

"That will be perfect. I'll tell him."

❧ ❧

Harriet and Emma took their mother home and warmed up some of the food people had brought them. Their mother was exhausted. After they'd eaten, Harriet took her upstairs to bed, lay down with her, and sang to her until she slept.

Desperate for time alone, Harriet went to her room, but Emma was in the next room. The old wall between their rooms was thin, and Harriet could not avoid hearing Emma talking on her cell phone, first to her husband, then her daughter, describing all the events of the day.

Harriet grabbed a sweatshirt, ran down the stairs and out the door.

The long twilight of midsummer was fading into dusk when she reached the track by the creek. A light breeze stirred the trees. As fast as she walked, she could not outpace the turmoil within her. Neal … She could stand her father dying; he was old and sick and difficult. But Neal …

Just ahead, she saw two points of rock above a cluster of tamarisk. Without intending to, she had come to her childhood sanctuary. She pushed through the tamarisk, climbed up and turned sideways to slip between the tall rocks, and dropped down into her niche.

Below her the creek swirled and gurgled, glinting in the last light of the day. Harriet drew her knees up to her chest and pushed her face down between them. Even the song of the water, the gentleness of the dusk, the quiet trees bending over the creek could not soothe her.

The experiences of the last week tumbled through her. Only a week ago she had lain in the high meadow under the ponderosa pines and realized that the bubbles communicated with her telepathically. But the message she received from them had left her more bewildered than before. Then the nursing home. And her father's death.

Too much. All at once. And now Neal wanted to see her. Before he died.

She remembered the last time she had seen him, coming out of church with Sarah five or six years ago. He had looked fine, hardly different than when she had worked for him except for a little gray around his temples. She hadn't greeted him then, hadn't spoken with him since the day he'd sent her away.

How could he die? It was impossible. The ache of her love for him and the loss of him, held back for thirty-two years, clawed through her, physical and intense. She squeezed her knees tighter and groaned aloud, turning her head from side to side.

How can I bear to see him—then lose him again?

Unless I sing to him … Does he want to live? Does he still love me?

Chapter 21

Neal

Heart pounding, Harriet stood at the front door of Neal's house. The hospice nurse answered her hesitant knock.

"Come in," she said, swinging the door wide. "You must be Harriet. Dr. Walker is expecting you. Go on up. His room is at the top of the stairs."

Harriet's heart continued to pound wildly as she climbed the stairs. She reached the top and stood in the open door of Neal's bedroom. It was a spare, spacious room. A double bed, covered with a blue and white quilt, was against one wall, a desk on the opposite wall. Neal lay in a reclining chair by the window, his legs up, his head resting back and turned toward her. His eyes were closed.

Barely breathing, Harriet gazed at him. He had been a big man, lean but strong and as tall as she. Now he was thin, shockingly thin, shrunken. One hand lay open on the arm of the chair. It seemed almost translucent in the light of the afternoon sun coming through the window. Blinking back her tears, she watched the slight rise and fall of his chest.

He sighed and opened his eyes.

"Harriet," he greeted her. "You came." His eyes were the same, and his smile, but his voice was weak and husky. He beckoned. "Come in. Pull that chair over and sit by me." He pushed a button on his recliner, bringing his legs down and his back straighter.

Harriet picked up the chair by the desk and came to sit beside him. He held out his hand to her. She took it in both of hers. She wanted to lay her cheek against it, kiss it, but she simply held it, soaking in the dear, familiar feel of him, unchanged in spite of his gauntness. The Song rose up in full force, showing her the inside of his ravaged body.

Wait, she whispered inwardly to the Song. Let me just touch him. She felt the Song recede.

She still hadn't spoken. Her throat was clogged with tears.

Neal seemed to understand. He looked into her face with the same caring gaze she had loved so long ago. "Thank you for coming. I'm glad to see you. It's been a long time. How are you?"

Harriet found her voice at last. "I'm … I'm okay. I'm glad to see you, too."

"You look well. I'd forgotten what beautiful eyes you have. You cut your hair."

"It's growing out again. My … former husband insisted I cut it. He thought I looked like a hippie."

"I heard you were married. And recently divorced. Was that hard?"

"Yes … but it wasn't a good marriage. I'm better off without him."

"He made you cut your hair. Fool. It was beautiful. It still is." Neal leaned forward and caressed her cheek and the side of her head, then drew his fingers out through her hair.

Harriet closed her eyes, drinking in his touch. Tears escaped.

"Dear Harriet, you're crying."

"I've missed you."

"Ah." He dropped back against the chair and lay breathing with difficulty. Harriet could see it had been an effort for him to lean forward. When his breath quieted, he reached for her hand again. "I'm so glad you came. I want to ask your forgiveness before I die." He stopped to take a few breaths. "I need to apologize for taking advantage of you when you were so young and innocent. It's been on my conscience. I know I caused you great sorrow when I sent you away. Then when you wouldn't greet me or look at me when we met in passing for all these years, I gathered it was far worse than I'd thought. I don't know what other damage I may have done."

Harriet straightened and brushed remaining tears from her cheek. "No damage. No apology needed," she said vehemently. "Those years with you were the best thing that ever happened to me. Where would I be now without you? A bitter cripple, running my father's shoe store. You gave me everything. Healing from the horse kick, support to go to college. My life path, which has been beautiful and rewarding for me." Harriet felt tears coming to her eyes again. She brushed them impatiently aside. "And … and your love … was the sweetest thing I've experienced in all my life."

"Ah, Harriet. You're still so pure and passionate."

He smiled, the same tender smile that she'd held in her memory through all the years. "It was an important time for me, too," he said. "You were such an ardent apprentice. I loved teaching you, watching you blossom. I loved you. I still do." He tightened his fingers around her hand. "The devotion, the passion you gave me—it's a rare thing for a man to receive such love. I knew I shouldn't. I knew it would break Sarah's heart if it became known, and I loved her, too, though differently. Never with the passion I felt for you. I couldn't resist you."

"You took a great risk. I didn't understand then. But you could have lost everything."

"It was worth the risk."

He coughed, then lay still, struggling to breathe. Harriet watched him anxiously, until his breathing settled. "I hope I'm not tiring you."

"No. Please don't go yet. You've been gone so long. It may be the last time I see you before I die."

Harriet's heart clenched. "I can't bear to think of you dying." Even though Harriet had told the Song to wait, it kept rising up in her, giving her glimpses into his body. She could hardly contain it, but she didn't want to let go of his hand. In spite of her urge to release the Song to heal all that she saw, she had not forgotten Mrs. Maloney's admonitions. She bent her head, letting her hair fall across her face to hide her struggle.

"Don't grieve," Neal said softly. "I've had a full life."

They were quiet together for a few minutes. Harriet gathered her courage. "If you weren't dying, what would you do with your life now?"

"If I weren't dying … I don't know. I've fought so hard to live, and finally I've had to give up. I've made my peace with it now. But if I weren't dying …" He tilted his head back, closed his eyes a moment, and took a long breath before he answered. "Well, I'd probably open my practice again. I've always loved my work. And there's need. But I wouldn't want to work full time. I'd want to make space to savor life, walk by the creek, sit in the garden, lie on my back on the earth and watch the clouds pass by."

He paused. "The hardest part is leaving everything. Everything. All the people I love, my children and grandchildren." He turned his head to look out the window. "And all the beauty of earth and sky, the trees, the stars …"

Harriet's heart ached at the sadness that crossed his face. She remembered how the stars had called her back.

"And now," he said, "I'm finding it hard to say good-bye to you, finding you again after so long a time."

The ache in Harriet's chest moved up to her throat and stopped her words.

He stroked her palm with his thumb. "Tell me about your practice. Roger told me you were full and overflowing. Has it been good for you? Do you like being a chiropractor?"

"I do." Harriet took a deep breath. "And my practice has become amazing. Can I tell you a strange story?"

"Sure. I love strange stories."

Realizing how indeed strange her story was, Harriet hesitated, but her longing to share everything with him as she used to overcame her doubt. The Song pressed against her hand. Still she held it back as she told him the whole story (except the suicide bit)—about the sciatica that nothing could heal, about her night walk, how she had fallen through the ice, the twenty-four hours of amnesia, and awaking healed, singing on the hillside, Tiger, and the gift of the Song.

"No kidding. This song came and you could see into the cat's body? And then—did you use it in your practice?"

"Yes. I do. And miracles happen every day." She went on to tell him about Celia, and little Jack, and Leonard's ankle, and Margaret Harris's baby.

Neal's face had brightened. He looked as if he were enjoying her stories. "If you're doing all those miracles, don't you get swamped?"

"I sure do. But we manage. I have an incredible office manager, Brenda. She's been with me for years. She handles a lot of it. But there's more than getting swamped." Harriet went on to describe in detail the apparition of Morna Morningstar until Neal was laughing, his eyes alight with their old mischievous sparkle. "And that's not all," Harriet went on. "There're the reporters. I sometimes have to climb out the back window at the end of the day."

Neal was still laughing. "I bet that's a sight."

Harriet laughed, too. "Fortunately no one sees me."

Neal's laughter triggered a spell of coughing. He rolled away from her. Harriet laid her hand on his back. Even though she still held back the surge of the Song, her touch seemed to soothe him. After a long and scary minute, his coughing ended with a sigh, and he turned back to her. "How often I've longed for something like your song," he said, "when there was nothing more I could do and my patient was still in pain. It's a great story. If only it were true. Then you could sing to me and make me well again."

"It *is* true." Harriet was shaken. He doesn't believe me, she thought. But how could he?

"No. It can't be. Don't we wish, though."

"It's true. I've never lied to you."

"No … you haven't."

Then he started coughing again, a long bout. He struggled to sit up. Harriet supported him, holding him close in her arms until the spasm passed. Gently, she eased him down. He lay limp against the back of the chair, his brow shiny with sweat.

The sun had moved away from the window, and the air coming through was cooler. Harriet found the button on the chair that brought his legs up and reclined the back. She brought him water, supported him to help him drink, then covered him with a fleece throw she found at the foot of his recliner.

"You need to rest now," she said.

He nodded, his chest still heaving. "But don't go yet. Stay a little longer."

Harriet sat beside him, her hand on his chest, soothing the difficult breathing. Her own breath was unsteady, her heartbeat leaping up into her throat. It's all right, she told herself. He wants to live. He even knows what he wants to do if he could live.

"Would you like me to sing to you a little while?" she asked him.

He turned his head toward her. She couldn't read the expression in his eyes. Was it hope? Did he believe her after all?

He smiled his sweet, tender smile. "Yes, I'd like that."

She drew her chair closer, laid her hands on his body and released the Song. It began softly, then gradually swelled to its fullest and deepest beauty. Neal closed his eyes. Harriet sang, moving her hands over his body, watching the Song touch all the ravaged places, watching his breath ease and deepen, his flesh fill out, the lines of pain disappear from his face.

She sang a long time, until the sun sank low in the sky and the peace of twilight came through the window. Neal slept. At last the healing was complete. The Song faded away. Harriet got up from her chair, bent and kissed his brow, then silently slipped out of the room.

Chapter 22

Proposal

It was after dark when Harriet set off for Boulder. Everything within her resisted leaving, but she had been out of the office four days last week, and, when she had checked in that morning, Brenda had told her she had a full schedule the next day.

What would you do anyway? she asked herself as she drove down the dark, two-lane road toward the highway. Would you be at his door first thing in the morning to ask how he was? She blushed at the thought.

No, this is better, she assured herself. I mustn't be too forward. I'll be back next weekend. I'll see him then. But maybe, when he realizes he's healed, he'll call.

Her apartment felt strange and empty after the closeness of living with Emma and her mother. She took a warm bath to calm herself, but when she was finally settled, she couldn't sleep. All she could think of was Neal. Over and over, she relived his words of love, his tender touch when he stroked her cheek and ran his fingers through her hair. Her body quivered with longing. And she could not stop hoping, planning.

He is well now. Sarah is gone. We could be lovers again. He only wants to work part time. I could move down and help him with his practice. Maybe … even … we could get married.

Then she scolded herself. Hush, you're making it all up. Go to sleep. You've got a full day tomorrow.

At last she slept. The bubbles danced in her dreams, their Song sweet and soothing. She woke remembering the new word she'd received the week before. *Kiria.*

She sat up in bed. "Kiria," she said softly, and felt an answering thread of melody. She pushed back the covers and hurried to her study to write it down. Why hadn't she written it down before? I have three words now, she thought—eliria, tirini, and kiria. They must have their own language even though they communicate with me telepathically. Why would they need language if they communicate telepathically?

Then her thoughts swerved. I wonder how Neal is feeling this morning. He must believe my story now. Will he call me? Her body throbbed with desire.

Pull yourself together, she admonished herself. You're not a teenager. Grow up.

But when she was dressed and starting to comb her hair, she remembered his touch again, and felt she would faint with longing.

Will he call? I could call him. No.

Only when she got to her office and became absorbed in the Song and the healing unfolding under her hands did her inner tumult subside.

Until lunch. Brenda set out their food on the little table in the back room, then handed Harriet a copy of the *Daily Camera* with a front page headline "Miraculous Healings at the Compassionate Care Nursing Home."

Harriet dropped into her chair. "Oh, no!"

"It came out last Tuesday morning while you were driving south," Brenda said. "I thought you ought to see it."

"Last Tuesday? That pest Joel Peterson showed up at my house Monday evening when I got home from talking with Mrs. Maloney, but I didn't tell him anything. Where did he get all this?"

The article filled the top one forth of the front page, continued on page six.

"Sounds like one of the attendants talked."

"Damn!" Harriet scanned the article.

"On Sunday afternoon," it said, "more than thirty elderly residents of the Compassionate Care Nursing Home laid down their crutches, stood up from their wheel chairs, and walked, freed by the song of Dr. Harriet Ellis, who had come to give a Sunday afternoon concert.

"'It was a total miracle,' said one of the attendants, speaking on condition of anonymity. Mrs. Ada Maloney RN, manager of Compassionate Care, had forbidden all of her employees to speak of the event. 'She gave a beautiful concert, mostly hymns,' the attendant reported. 'Then one woman fell down after the concert. Dr. Ellis knelt beside her, her name was Lydia, and Dr. Ellis sang to her, a different kind of singing, kind of strange like a foreign language and like she had more than one voice, but even more beautiful than how she sang in the concert. When she finished, Lydia got up and walked without her cane. Then Dr. Ellis touched everyone in the room, one after another, and sang to them, and they were all healed, walking and skipping and laughing and crying and hugging each other. It was the most amazing thing I have ever seen. I'll never forget it as long as I live.' The attendant had tears in her eyes as she spoke.

"Neither Maloney or Ellis would comment.

"Dr. Ellis's neighbor, Leah Cohen, said she didn't know Dr. Ellis very well, but that she had healed Cohen's cat last January. 'He was dying,' Cohen said. 'The vet wanted to put him down, but I couldn't bear to. I asked Harriet to sit with him while I went to get his medicine, and when I got back he was asleep in her lap and she was singing a real pretty song to him. Then when he woke up, he was all better. I don't know what she did, but he's fine now.'"

The article went on to report that many of the residents were leaving Compassionate Care because they were all well.

Harriet dropped the paper on the floor beside her chair. "Crimminy!"

She looked over at Brenda, feeling her belly roil. "What else has happened here since I've been gone?"

"A lot more phone calls. I put a message on your voice mail, saying you'd had a death in the family and the office was closed until today. But I didn't do that until after the article came out. I came in Wednesday to catch up a little, and your voice mail was full. I took it all down, and it was full again this morning. So I've got a lot of folks lined up and all those from last week put in this week, and everyone else pushed ahead a week."

Harriet put her elbow on the table and dropped her head in her hand.

"Don't worry, honey." Brenda patted her shoulder. "I'll handle it. You're just going to do your regular schedule like you always have, and one appointment a day for emergencies."

"Any more reporters hanging around?"

"Yeah, several, the day I was in the office. I just kept the door locked and they finally went away. No one's come today. It'll blow over like that story about Jack did. Now never mind all that. Tell me about your family and the funeral and all."

Harriet startled, disoriented, as if she were on a bungee cord, bouncing up and down and swinging wildly in all directions. Her thoughts had been all of Neal. Now the newspaper article. But, of course, her father had just died, and, as far as Brenda was concerned, that had been the main event of the last week.

She had never told Brenda about Neal. Never told anyone. Her mother would remember, if reminded, that she had worked for Neal when she was in high school. Nan might suspect something. She remembered rumors that Harriet had had a crush on her father long ago. But no one knew that Neal had been her lover and was still the most important person in her whole life. No one.

So as she ate slowly, trying to calm the chaos in her belly, Harriet told Brenda about the funeral, her mother, her sisters, and how kind and helpful Reverend Harvey had been. Then just as she gathered up her cup and plate to return to work, Brenda said, "Oh, I almost forgot. You got a call this morning from a Dr. Walker in Cottonwood Creek. He wanted you to call him back, left his number. He didn't want an appointment. Dr. Walker, who's he?"

The cup and plate dropped from Harriet's hands and crashed onto the linoleum floor. Fortunately they were plastic and empty.

"Oh," Harriet gasped, hiding her face behind her hair as she bent to pick up her dishes. "He … he's an old friend. Thanks for taking the call. Where's his number?"

"Somewhere on my desk. But it's almost one thirty. I need to let your next person in. Dr. Walker said it wasn't an emergency; he just wanted to talk. You can call him after you get done today."

❧ ❧

Harriet sat on her bed, the phone on the nightstand beside her. She still knew by heart the phone number of Neal's office, but she had never called his home. The piece of paper with his home phone number quivered in her hand.

Three rings, then his voice. "Harriet, I'm so glad you called. I've been thinking of you all day."

His voice, his dear voice, clear and strong. He sounded like himself again. Harriet felt the doors of her heart swing wide open, her love pour out to him. She held her breath a moment before daring to speak.

"I've been thinking of you, too. How are you feeling?"

"How am I feeling? I'm alive! I feel fantastic. The cancer's gone. I know. Not only that, but I feel young and strong. I haven't felt so good in years, maybe never. *What did you do?* Is your story true after all? That strange, beautiful singing?"

"It's true."

"But how? Is it true you fell through the ice and don't know how you got out? But then your sciatic pain was gone, and you could sing and heal, see into the body, all those things you told me?"

"It's all true."

"How could it be? But how else could I feel like this when only yesterday I was coughing so hard I thought I might die in your arms? Harriet, I'm blown away."

"I am, too. Still. Though it's been five months since it all began. I still don't understand, but I'm getting some clues. I didn't tell you all of it. There's lots more."

"I want to hear all of it. I want to see you. Are you coming back to Cottonwood Creek soon? Shall I drive up to Boulder?"

"I'll be back to Cottonwood Creek next weekend. I need to check on my mother."

"Of course. That's right. I've been so excited about seeing you again and now feeling all new, I'd forgotten. Your dad died. How are you doing with that? I didn't even ask you last night."

"I'm doing okay. We were never close."

"I remember that."

"He'd been sick a long time. I knew he was dying, but still it sort of upended me. And I'm concerned about my mother."

"Couldn't you heal him?"

"No. He wouldn't let me. It isn't I who heals, it's the Song. And he wouldn't let it in. It would bounce back when I touched him."

"Bounce back?"

"Yes. That happened with one of my patients, too. He didn't want to be healed. Or it wasn't right."

Harriet felt a rush of joy and relief. Neal was there. She could talk to him as she used to, those years long ago when he was teaching her. He would help her understand.

"Neal," she said in a burst. "There's so much I want to talk with you about. About healing. How much should we intervene? That's always been a question, but now the Song makes such huge changes. How much healing is the responsibility of the patient? Eliza quit her practice because she got tired of people taking no responsibility, just coming in three times a week, lying on the table and waiting to be fixed. You should have heard her, a long rant."

Neal chuckled. "Knowing Eliza, I can imagine."

"And maybe someone's pain is part of their path, their karma, or God's will, and if we fix it, then they don't learn the lesson the pain had for them."

"Those are good questions."

"Weekend before last, the Song healed almost everyone in a nursing home, and then the head nurse told me I shouldn't interrupt their dying process."

"Wait! You healed everyone in a nursing home? That must have been a scene."

"It was. There was one woman who told me not to sing for her. She said. 'Let me go.' She died the next day. So yesterday—when I was with you—I wouldn't release the Song until you told me how sad you were that you were dying."

"I'm glad to be alive. Though I had made my peace with dying. I felt complete with everyone except you. I'm so grateful you came yesterday." He paused. A long silence on the phone line. "I've missed you," he said at last. "I never thought you'd cut me off so completely. Why did you turn your head away, every time I greeted you when we passed in town or at church? I'd hoped we could still be friends. I wanted to know how your work was going. Your life. I got news only through gossip. You could have come and consulted with me. That would have been acceptable."

"I … I couldn't." Even though she was alone, Harriet felt herself blushing. "It would have been too hard not to beg you to make love to me. And I didn't want to make trouble, start rumors."

"Maybe you were right. I might have had trouble restraining myself, especially if you had asked me. Ah, sweetheart, we'll make up for lost time now. When you come down, let's take a long walk by the creek. I am so eager to see you again, hear the rest of your story, catch up with all the years we've been apart."

Harriet's heart was pounding, tears coming to her eyes. "I'd love to walk by the creek with you."

"I want to drop an idea in your head. I've been thinking about it all day. What I said yesterday about only working part time—It was hypothetical then, but now I do want to reopen my practice, but also to make space to savor life. Now that it's given back, it feels so precious. So what I'm leading up to is a proposal. Would you consider coming back to Cottonwood Creek to practice with me? I know you're doing well up there in Boulder." He hesitated. "But it was what you wanted long ago."

Harriet closed her eyes and leaned her head back. She couldn't speak. A huge wave of grief, longing, hope poured through her—grief for all the years lost, longing to touch him, hold him, love him again, and hope that at last her longing could be fulfilled.

"Harriet?"

"I'm here." She drew in a breath. "I would like that. I'd need to transition."

"Of course. We'll talk about that, too, when you come."

Harriet heard another voice in the background.

"My nurse is calling me to dinner," Neal said. "I haven't dismissed her yet. We'll talk soon. Goodnight, sweetheart."

"Goodnight."

Chapter 23

On The Creek Road

All the next day, Harriet's heart was dancing with joy. Under and around the Song and working with her patients, she was seeing Neal's eyes, his tender smile, imagining walking on the creek road with him. Would he hold her hand? Imagining stopping by the little yellow house to check it out—and making love in the treatment room as they had long ago.

At lunch, Brenda asked. "What's going on with you? You're all bubbly and distracted. You've been dropping things. That's not like you."

Harriet smiled across the table at Brenda. Trust Brenda to notice. "I am kind of excited," she admitted. "I got an offer last night from Dr. Walker. He's a chiropractor down in Cottonwood Creek. He's in his seventies, and wants to start working part time. He invited me to come down there and join his practice."

"No kidding! That would be a big change. Are you considering it?"

"I am. I could move in with my mother and look after her. And I like Cottonwood Creek. It's quiet and rural and people are friendly. I don't like Boulder as much as I used to. It's gotten so much bigger, more traffic, not so friendly. And I … really like Dr. Walker. I worked in his office when I was in high school and he was kind to me, helped me get started."

"Does he know what you're doing?"

"I told him."

Brenda looked at Harriet over the top of her glasses. "Are you running away? From all the attention, the reporters?"

Too full of the real reason for going, Harriet didn't know what to say. An unruly giggle bubbled up in her throat. She pressed it down and shook her head.

"Honey, you know running away is not going to help," Brenda persisted. "Even if you go down there and don't tell anyone where you're going, doing what you do, people are gonna find you soon enough."

"I know. But there aren't so many people in Cottonwood Creek."

Brenda raised an eyebrow. Harriet's giggle escaped. She blushed and pulled herself together. "I do want to keep an eye on my mother. And I feel ready for a change. Would you come with me? I can't imagine my practice without you."

"Doesn't this Dr. Walker already have an office manager?"

"No. He's been sick for a while, and is just now ready to reopen his practice."

"You healed him?"

"Yes."

"So he really does know what you do. Does he realize his practice is gonna go through a radical change?"

"I'm not sure. I'm going down next weekend to check on my mom, and we'll talk it over some more then."

Brenda shifted in her chair. "Now, about me going with you—Where is this Cottonwood Creek? The only thing that might hold me up is if I were too far from my kids and grandkids."

"Southeast of Denver, about a two hour drive from here."

"I could get there faster on my Hog."

"Parker's the nearest city. It's about an hour from there, out on the plains."

"Parker! That's where my youngest lives, Michael and his family. Cottonwood Creek would be closer to them than here. I like it down there. I've actually considered moving there in the far future when we retire." She grinned and patted Harriet's hand. "Sure, I can go with you.

We're a team. After thirty plus years … I can't imagine your practice without me, either."

"Thank you! Thank you!" Harriet jumped up from her chair to embrace Brenda, bumping the table and slopping her glass of lemonade.

"There you go again, bumping and spilling." Brenda patted Harriet's shoulder. "Calm down now. We can't go today. We'll have to wrap things up here. There's gonna be some long faces."

That evening Harriet wanted to call Neal to tell him Brenda could come with her, but she felt hesitant. Maybe he would call her. She ate her dinner, and hung around, restless, unable to focus on anything. Don't be silly, she admonished herself. He didn't say he'd call. Just that we'd talk next weekend.

Finally, when it was late enough that it was unlikely he'd call, she left her condo and drove to the lake, hoping a twilight walk would calm her down.

It was a lovely evening, dusk moving to darkness, a young moon hanging low over the ridge, the smell of Russian olive blossoms sweet on the air. Harriet walked swiftly, but was unable to outpace a growing anxiety, a sense that something was wrong. She reached out with her thought, with her love, to Neal and felt—nothing, blank. She returned home, still anxious, and slept badly. The bubbles did not sing to her that night.

The next day in the office, the Song still poured through, the healing still unfolded, the trance was still sweet, but fear moved like a dark worm within her.

"I don't know what's wrong with me," she told Brenda at lunch. "I feel worried."

"You've got a lot of change coming up," Brenda said. "Don't worry. It's all gonna work out okay. I'll be with you, like I was when we moved up here."

There was a message on her voice mail when Harriet got home. Her fingers trembled as she dialed the number for her message box. *Probably my mother,* she thought, trying to dampen her hope that it would be Neal.

It was a message from Nan Walker. Her voice sounded shaky. She said only, "Please call me," and left her number.

Nan! From the sound of her voice, something must be wrong. Harriet drew in her breath, sat down in her desk chair, and dialed Nan's number.

"Harrie." Nan's voice was even shakier than it had been in her message. "I'm glad you called. I thought you'd want to know. Dad died last night."

"Died?" The dark fear that had lain in Harriet's gut all day exploded and immersed her. "I thought … I thought he was better. I talked to him the other night. He said he was … in remission …"

"He was. It was like a miracle. We were so happy he'd be with us awhile longer. But it wasn't the cancer that killed him. It was Dave Miller's crazy kid, Arby. He was off-roading in his dad's pickup on that track by the creek, he and another kid, drunk. That road's not fit to drive on anyway. Dad was walking there. He always liked to walk by the creek." Nan's voice broke in a sob. "Damn fool kid went careening around a sharp bend and hit him. Hit him and drove on. Dad was going to come to our house for dinner. When he didn't show, we went looking for him. And found him lying by the side of the road, crushed."

Nan stopped talking. The sound of her weeping came over the phone line. The image of Neal lying crushed on the road hit Harriet like a blow in the solar plexus. She gasped and curled over.

Nan swallowed her sobs and spoke again. "He was conscious. He told us not to grieve, his time had come. He said your name, too, but we couldn't catch all of his words. Then he died right there on the road."

Nan wept again. Harriet doubled up in her desk chair, her face between her knees, the phone still pressed to her ear.

Nan's voice came through. "The funeral will be next Saturday. I thought you might want to come."

"Yes." Somehow Harriet managed to speak. "I'll be there. I'm so sorry. Thank you for letting me know."

She did not remember hanging up the phone. Shock turned her to ice. Her consciousness fled away into blackness. Hours later, she found herself curled up on the floor under her desk, the room dark.

⊸ *Chapter 24* ⊸

The Song Ends

It was eight o'clock when Harriet woke the next morning. Sometime during the night she had crawled into bed. Feeling blurred and crumpled, she sat up, looked at the clock, and sucked in her breath. Her first patient was scheduled at the office in one hour.

I can't, she thought. I can't sing the Song ever again.

All the doubts and fears about her work descended on her like a tornado, whirling her out of her center, battering her with debris.

I can't. I don't know what I'm doing. I shouldn't have sung to Neal. His time had come. He told me he was at peace. Then he died a horrible death being hit by a truck. I'm selfish. I just wanted him to be strong again so he could be my lover.

She flung herself down on the bed, pulled a pillow over her head. Her thoughts raced on. I'm unworthy of the Song. I always have been. Maybe I only used it to feel important. I'm not important. I don't understand the Song. It's so strange. I'm a kook. What was I thinking? I don't know what's best for all those patients who came to me. How do I know if someone's time has come? It's too much power.

The thought of the power of the Song sent a wave of panic through her. Power to heal a cat, a baby with leukemia, to let a cripple walk again, power to dispel a tumor, to bring someone back to life who was dying. Who was she to channel such power?

I'm crazy. I can't do it anymore, ever again. She pushed the pillow aside and rolled onto her stomach, face down.

201

A thread of melody wove through her. Then the Song came, sweet and strong, filled with compassion. *Ah.*

"No!" Harriet arched up and slammed her fists down on the bed. "Stop. Go away. Leave me alone. Just let me be normal again."

An image came. She was standing in the center of a circular space with windows all around her. The Song came again, aching with love, then faded away. One by one the windows darkened, until there was no light left.

Harriet opened her eyes. She was in her bedroom, her fists still clenched. Daylight came through her window.

Then the loss of Neal and all her hopes and dreams inundated her. She curled into a ball and wept. Horrible wrenching sobs, tearing through her like claws.

After what seemed a long time, she quieted and looked at the clock again. Eight forty-five. She should be at her office. She pushed herself up to sitting. What shall I do? I can't sing the Song. They've all been waiting for their appointments, waiting for miracles. I can't do miracles without the Song.

Her hands shook as she picked up the phone by her bed and dialed the office.

Brenda answered on the first ring. "Hi, honey. Where are you? It's just about time for your first."

"I can't," was all Harriet could get out.

"What's up? What do you mean you can't. Can't what?"

"Can't come in. Can't sing the Song anymore."

"Honey, what's wrong? You sound awful."

"I'm sick."

"Oh, my God." Brenda sounded distressed. "There's twelve people lined up for today, waiting for your Song. I'd better start phoning. You rest. I'll stop in on you later."

Harriet lay down on the bed again. Her bedroom window was open. Outside it was a fresh summer morning. Bird calls and a sweet flower scent came in on a light breeze. Dappled sunlight and leaf shadows danced across her bed.

Inside Harriet, all was darkness and bitter cold. She pulled her pillow over her head. She curled up so tightly that it hurt, squeezed her eyes shut. But nothing could shut out the stabbing grief in her gut, the agony of her loss. She willed herself away into darkness.

Much later the doorbell rang. The sound barely penetrated Harriet's blackness. She burrowed deeper under her pillow. The bell rang again. Then again. Harriet held her breath, waiting for it to stop.

"Harriet." Brenda's voice. "Harriet, are you there? Let me in." The sound of fists thumping on the door. "Harriet." Louder. More thumping.

Brenda. She wouldn't go away. She'd find some way to break in if Harriet didn't open the door.

Harriet uncurled. Every cell in her body ached. She stumbled to the front door and fumbled with the lock.

Brenda came in with a burst of summer sunlight. "Oh, my God, honey. What happened to you? You look terrible. Here, come sit down."

Brenda's warm, plump hand leading her to the couch. Brenda's arm around her.

Harriet sat within its curve, hunched and silent.

"Honey, talk to me. What's wrong?" Brenda's hand caressing her head. Brenda's love pouring over her.

Harriet found her voice. "Neal … Dr. Walker died Tuesday night. I didn't know till last night."

"Dr. Walker? The one who was asking you to join his practice down in Cottonwood Creek? He died? Just after you made him all well?"

"Yes." Harriet's words came out in short bursts. "Sunday he was dying. Of cancer. I sang to him. Then he was well again. You know. Like Margaret Harris's baby."

"I know. Then he asked you to come down and join his practice, and you were stoked to do it. Then he died. Did the cancer come back?"

"No. He was run over by a drunken kid in a pickup truck when he was walking by the creek." Harriet choked on a smothered sob.

"That's terrible. Of course you're upset." Brenda shifted to look into Harriet's face. "But there's something more. What were you saying that you can't sing the Song anymore?"

"Don't you get it?" Harriet pulled out of Brenda's embrace. Impatience tinged with rage overtook her. "He's dying. The Song heals him. It's the Song. I know it's not me. But it comes through me. I'm responsible. Then two days later he's dead anyway. He told his daughter his time had come, and I'm sitting there healing him. Don't you get it?"

She grabbed Brenda by the shoulders. "I don't know what I'm doing. I messed up. Maybe I'm messing up with every healing I'm doing. Like Mrs. Maloney at Compassionate Care said. Maybe I sang to Neal … Dr. Walker just because …"

Harriet stopped. Her promise of secrecy bound her still.

"Easy, honey. Easy." Brenda laid her hand on Harriet's knee. "You're not messing up. I've been watching you and all your patients for months now, and what I see is you're bringing joy and ease into all those peoples' lives. That's a good thing. And if someone doesn't want to be healed, the Song bounces back like it did with your dad and that guy Ron. And if someone's time has come, like your friend what's-his-name, Dr. Walker, and you heal him, he dies anyway. You haven't done any harm. Maybe you did something really good. He had two good days after you healed him. Maybe he needed those days to complete something, and you gave him the chance. You don't know."

Harriet pounded the couch with her fist. "That's just it. I don't know. I don't know anything. I don't know what I'm going to do. I can't sing the Song anymore, and now I have this reputation. Everyone who comes to me expects it. If I do just a regular chiropractic adjustment, they'll be disappointed. They'll be mad. I can't show my face."

"I don't know why you can't sing the Song. It's clear you need to rest today, but I haven't canceled tomorrow. There's a bunch of folks scheduled who are suffering and pinning their hopes on you."

"Brenda, I can't." Harriet jumped up off the couch and paced the length of the small room. "I'm scared. It's too much power. I'm faulty. I make mistakes. It's too weird. How did it ever happen to me anyway? I still don't know."

"I don't know either." Brenda's brow was furrowed with concern as she looked up at Harriet standing on the other side of the room, her fists clenched. "Maybe we'll never know. But the Song is a gift. I'm sure of that. Not only to your patients, but to you. Look how you just jumped up and strode across the room. You couldn't have done that six months ago. Your sciatica is healed. And I've never, in all the years I've known you, seen you so happy as you've been lately, your face all shiny when you come out between clients, your eyes peaceful. Never you mind that Mrs. Maloney. Her orderly world's been upset, and some folks just can't stand that."

Harriet's fists were clenched so tightly they ached. She saw again the circular room, the windows going dark. "It doesn't matter," she said. "The Song is gone." In that moment, she realized it truly was. Panic, deeper than the panic that had caused her to send it away, swept through her, an emptiness without bottom. The room spun.

Brenda's voice penetrated the void. "It can't be. Come sit by me." She patted the couch beside her.

Harriet went to her, the only source of warmth she could perceive in the emptiness. Brenda took her hand. "Look here. I sprained my wrist yesterday picking up a heavy flower pot. Nothing serious. But if you would just sing a moment and put it right, I'd really appreciate it."

Harriet took Brenda's wrist in her hand. The wrist was slightly swollen and she could feel that one of the small bones was out of place. She couldn't see inside. The Song did not come. Automatically, with the skills she had honed for decades, she gently manipulated the wrist and settled the misplaced bone. When she finished, the wrist was still swollen. Even after the adjustment, it would take time to heal—in the old way, the normal way.

Harriet lifted her head and looked into Brenda's eyes. "It's gone," she said.

"My wrist feels better anyway," Brenda said. But Harriet could see the shock in Brenda's eyes.

Chapter 25

Confession

*H*arriet stood, numb and still, at the outer edge of the group gathered around Neal's grave. She was vaguely aware of summer sun hot on her back, the low murmur of the creek, the smell of freshly turned earth. The casket had been lowered into the hole. Reverend Harvey was talking, quoting Scripture and speaking of the afterlife, but Harriet couldn't take in his words.

Somehow she'd managed to pull herself together enough to drive down to Cottonwood Creek and pretend to her mother that she was okay. She'd managed to keep control even when Nan told her there wouldn't be a viewing because Neal had been so bashed up. She'd held it together through the service in the church, but now, standing by the grave, she found herself beginning to tremble, her whole body rigid with denial. Neal couldn't be dead. He couldn't be.

Reverend Harvey had stopped speaking. Looking between the people clustered in front of her, Harriet saw Nan and Roger and their spouses and children come forward to scatter handfuls of earth on the casket. She clenched her jaw, held her breath. Then when Roger and Nan's husband picked up shovels and began to throw whole shovelsful down into the hole, Harriet broke.

She spun and ran away from the group around the grave, away from the grave. She tore across the cemetery toward a clump of junipers at the far western edge. Only when she reached it did she realize it sheltered her father's grave. The earth was still raw under her feet, but she noticed, even in her grief, that someone had scattered grass seed over it.

She hesitated only a moment, then ran behind the junipers, out of sight of the rest of the graveyard, and flung herself on the ground. Sobs came, deep, racking, unbearable, rending her.

Much later, when she had cried until she could cry no more, as she lay numb and broken, the harsh prairie grass rough under her cheek, she heard footsteps approaching, then a rustle in the grass as someone knelt beside her. She felt a warm, gentle hand on her back.

"Harriet?" It was Winston. "Can I help you?"

Harriet stirred and sat up. She felt the wetness of tears and snot and the roughness of bits of dried grass on her cheeks. With the heel of her hand, she rubbed her face, smearing it all. She drew in a ragged breath. "Do you have a handkerchief?" she asked.

"I do." He reached into his pocket and handed her a soft, smooth white square of cloth, neatly folded.

Harriet wiped her cheeks and blew her nose. "Thank you." She crumpled the handkerchief in her hand.

"Will you come with me?" Winston asked. "Everyone's gone."

"Okay."

Harriet pushed herself up to standing. Her vision was blurred and her feet felt far away and disconnected. She made a brief attempt to brush bits of grass and juniper needles off her navy-blue dress, stumbled.

"Take my arm," Winston offered.

She slipped her hand into the bend of his elbow. The bones of his forearm were strong and firm under her fingers.

Slowly they walked across the cemetery. Winston led her on a path to the parking lot that did not pass Neal's grave. Harriet kept her head bent, focusing on each step. Everything felt unreal.

At the church, the reception was going on in the fellowship hall, and there were people milling around the front door. Harriet cringed.

"Let's go this way." Winston led her in a side door and up to his office. He seated her on his couch and brought her a glass of water. "I need to make an appearance downstairs," he said. "For just a little while. Rest here. I'll be back soon."

"I don't want to bother you," Harriet began.

"Please, Harriet. Wait for me. I don't know what has hit you so hard, but please let me help you. We're friends. I care about you. A lot."

"Okay. I'll wait."

Winston left. Harriet curled up on the couch. Its plush finish was dark green, smoother under her cheek than prairie grass. She remembered sitting there the night of her birthday party, cradling little Lucia in her arms, rocked in the sweet trance of the Song as she watched the last traces of Lucia's burns fade away.

That was good, she thought. There's no question that was good. I'm glad she didn't have to grow up scarred. Comforted by that thought, she nestled deeper into the couch. She was exhausted. Perhaps she dozed. She wasn't sure.

Sometime later, Winston came in. Harriet sat up. She still had his handkerchief crumbled in her hand.

Winston pulled up a chair and sat facing her. "How are you doing?"

The compassion in his eyes, the kindness in his voice almost undid her again. She tightened her jaw. "A little better."

"That's good. Would you talk to me? Tell me what it is that has upset you so? I know it's been tough for a lot of people, losing two long-time pillars of this town in as many weeks. Did coming to another funeral bring back the pain of your father's death?"

"No. That's not it."

Harriet felt as if a tsunami was rising in her. Her secret, held so many years, was too huge, too unbearable to contain any longer. "Can I trust you?" she blurted. "I have a secret. No one must ever know."

Winston leaned forward and took both her hands in his. He looked directly into her eyes. "You can trust me. I can keep a secret."

"It's Neal. Dr. Walker." Harriet's words came out in short bursts. "I loved him more than anyone in my whole life. He was dying of cancer and last Sunday I sang to him and he was healed. And he wasn't married anymore and we were finally going to be able to be together. I was so happy. Then he was run over and he's dead. He told Nan his time had come. His time had come, and still I sang to him. Because I didn't want him to die. But it was wrong. Because his time had come. And now the Song has gone away. It's gone."

Harriet closed her eyes. A wave of nausea swept through her. She clung to Winston's warm, strong hands.

"That's a lot at once," he said. "Tell me one piece at a time. Tell me why you loved Neal so much."

Tears rose again. Her lips trembled. She pressed back the tears, looked straight into Winston's eyes, and poured out her story—the two and a half years of her adolescence in which her relationship to Neal had transformed her life, her eighteenth summer when they were lovers, her dream of working with him once she got her degree, the long years of separation, the hope that had blossomed when the Song healed him, the shock of his death.

At the end she broke down, sobbing. "I can't bear it that he's dead. Gone. Lying there with earth on top of him."

As her story unfolded, Winston's eyes had widened in astonishment, but there was no judgment in them. He sat quietly with her until her sobs subsided. "No wonder your heart is broken," he said. "And there is still more. You said the Song was gone."

"Yes." She told him about Compassionate Care, Olivia, and Mrs. Maloney's lecture. "So I shouldn't have sung to Neal. His time had come. Like Olivia. I knew. I felt death in the room with him. He said he was at peace. But I wanted to be with him again, so I sang anyway. Then when I heard about his death, I knew I'd done it wrong. So I told the Song to go away. So I wouldn't make more mistakes. And it did. It's gone."

"Is it really gone. Are you sure?"

"Yes. Brenda asked me to sing to her sprained wrist. I tried, but the Song didn't come. So I adjusted it the old way."

"You could still do that?"

"Of course. I've been doing chiropractic for over thirty years. But now everyone expects miracles of me. I can't sing in church ever again either. I'd just have an ordinary voice."

"No, you mustn't try to sing tomorrow. Just come and receive the comfort of the service."

Harriet opened the crumpled handkerchief and blew her nose again. "I've messed up your nice hanky. I'll wash it and bring it back to you."

Winston smiled. "Don't worry about the handkerchief. How are you feeling now?"

Harriet let out a short breath. "Better, actually," she said in surprise. "It's such a relief to be able to tell someone … all of that."

"Know that your story is safe with me."

"I do know."

"You look very tired. I want to think about all you've told me. Can we talk again? Take our Sunday afternoon walk tomorrow?"

"Yes. I'd like that."

"May I walk you home?"

"Yes. Thank you. I'm still kind of wobbly."

The sun was low and slanting when they set out from the church. The reception was over, all the cars and people dispersed. They walked slowly, mostly in silence, Harriet leaning on Winston's arm.

Walking by The Creek

It was cloudy on Sunday afternoon, cooler than the day before. Harriet met Winston at the manse and they walked together toward the creek. Harriet was feeling calmer. She'd gone to church with her mother that morning and then spent some time going over paperwork relating to her father's death.

But when they reached the creek track, she stopped. A wave of grief swept her. She pressed her hand over her mouth, holding back tears. "I don't know if I can walk on this road again," she said to Winston, "since Neal …"

Winston put his arm gently around her shoulders. "From what you've told me of Neal, I don't think he would want you to give up all this beauty, all that walking here means to you."

Harriet took a deep breath. The wave of grief subsided, leaving her slightly nauseated. "You're right. He wouldn't. And I would miss it terribly."

"Come then. There's a memorial about a half mile down the road. People have put flowers there where Neal was hit. Shall we add some?" He gestured to the wildflowers growing in abundance along the sides of the track and the creek.

Harriet nodded. They walked in silence, stopping from time to time to gather flowers.

The memorial was just past a sharp curve in the road. Someone had put up a small cross, and numerous bouquets of faded flowers were clustered around it. Harriet knelt and laid her offering at the foot of the cross, then bent forward, pressing her brow into the warm, dry dirt. Here he had lain dying and told Nan his time had come. And spoken Harriet's name. Grief too deep for tears crushed her, an aching so painful it took her breath away.

After a while she felt a hand on her back. "Harriet?"

She uncurled and sat back on her heels. Winston was squatting beside her, his eyes full of concern.

She caught a few quick, short breaths. "It comes in waves."

"Yes."

Harriet remembered how Winston had spoken of his wife who died two years ago in an automobile accident. He knows, she thought.

She stood. "I can go on now."

They continued down the road, their long legs in matching stride. The colors of leaves, flowers, and water were muted under the gray sky. The sound of the creek rippled beside them, and the fragrance of Russian olives in bloom floated around them.

After a while, Winston said, "I want to hear more about the bubbles and the Song. I know you sent the Song away, but before that—did you get any more messages?"

Harriet had to pause a moment to pull that thread out of the tangle of recent events. "Yes. I did. It was only two weeks ago when I was out on a hike—though with all that's happened since it feels like years."

"Tell me."

She told Winston how she'd begun to sing to the bubbles the way they sang to her, and her realization that they were communicating telepathically. She told him she'd asked the question about underlying causes and their astonishing answer. *On Eliria there is no pain.*

Winston stopped walking. "Are you sure they said *on* Eliria?"

"Yes."

"On, not in?"

"I think so."

Winston started walking again. Harriet moved into step beside him. After a while, he said, "Have you considered the possibility your bubbles might be extraterrestrials?"

"Extraterrestrials? Brenda suggested that, too. I *have* wondered, more lately, but I still don't see how they could be extraterrestrials. We know there's no other life in the solar system and everything else is light years away. How would they get here?"

"It's a vast universe. I'm quite sure there is more going on out there among the stars than we can possibly imagine. I could imagine there is a place in the universe where there is no pain, where beings communicate telepathically, where all communication is healing and love."

"Do you really think there could be such a place?"

"I only said I could imagine it—from what you've told me about the bubbles and from what I've experienced of the Song."

Harriet ached with longing. "Could there be? But how would beings from such a place get here? It's so far."

"If they could create something as miraculous as the Song, maybe they could also create a way of moving through light years. I don't know. It's just a thought. But now I want to know about the Song leaving you, not being there when you held Brenda's wrist. What happened?"

"I was really upset. Scared of using the power of it wrong. Like I told you. They started singing to me to comfort me, and I just yelled at them. Told them to go away and let me be normal again. They sang to me one more time, no message … except love. Then they were gone, and I haven't heard from them since."

"How does it feel to have them gone, the Song gone?"

Harriet went inside and felt again the terrible moment when all the windows went dark. "It feels empty," she said. "I thought I'd be relieved, but I'm not. It's a loss, a huge loss. It's hard to think of going on without the Song. As if I don't even know who I am anymore without it. I didn't realize how much it had become a part of me."

"Do you think you could call to them and ask for it back?"

"I don't know. All the reasons I sent it away are still there. I don't know why they chose me. I don't feel worthy." Harriet bent her head.

"Not worthy!" Winston turned to Harriet and put his hands on her shoulders. "Harriet, look at me."

Harriet lifted her head and looked into his eyes. His hands were warm and gentle on her shoulders.

"I want you to hear me," he said. "Believe what I say. I can't think of anyone more worthy, more perfect to receive the Song. You have a true and loving heart. You are exceptionally compassionate, and the focus of all your adult life has been to be of service. You are also unusually intelligent and sensitive. And what's more, you are skilled and licensed in a culturally acceptable healing practice. You are the perfect person to receive the Song. And what you have to give with it is so needed."

Harriet felt abashed by Winston's words. Knowing no way to acknowledge them, she took off on another track. "But what if I'm interfering with God's will for the people the Song heals? Maybe He is punishing them."

"God is love." Winston said. "I can't believe God punishes us. In my opinion, punishment is a perverted human idea projected onto God by priests of various persuasions to hold power through fear. Our suffering is the result of our own straying from the path."

"What about what we call 'acts of God'—drought, fire, flood? What about innocent people hurt by those who stray from the path?" Harriet and Winston had been standing in the middle of the road, facing each other. Winston took her arm and led her to a soft grassy place by the creek bank.

"Let's sit down," he said. "We are now confronting the age-old question: How can an all-powerful God of love allow the misery that we endure on Earth? I don't know the answer."

"We learn from suffering, I suppose." Another wave of aching grief swept her. Am I learning from this? she asked herself.

"It's true," Winston said. "Suffering is a strong teacher. And sometimes it takes suffering to turn us to God. But, Harriet, we are not called to create suffering; there's plenty of that on this Earth. We are called to heal, in whatever way we can. You know. That's why you became a chiropractor. Why I became a minister. So, no, I don't think you are interfering with God's will when you heal through the Song. Any more than you are when you heal with your traditional chiropractic skills. You are just much more effective."

Harriet sat silent, watching the flow of the creek, remembering the ecstasy of the Song and the joy she'd had in being able to heal all that ailed her patients. After a while she asked, "Do you think I should try to call them and ask for the Song to be given back?"

"It's not for me to say. It's a huge gift. And a huge responsibility. But I did think you were happy with it. And I know it has been healing to many. I don't know the stories of all the people you have healed up in Boulder, but I know about little Lucia, and your mother, and how my whole congregation is blessed by your singing. I'm sad to think I would never hear it again."

Harriet picked up little sticks out of the grass, broke them into even lengths, and arranged them in patterns.

"I wonder if they really are extraterrestrials," she said at length. "If maybe they come from a planet called Eliria. That was the first word they gave me. That would be very strange."

"Indeed."

"Maybe we should stop calling them bubbles. It's not very respectful. Maybe we should call them Elirians."

"We could do that."

"Winston, are we nuts?"

"Maybe." He smiled and laid his hand over hers. "Maybe we would be wise to keep this just between ourselves for now. Wait and see."

Chapter 27

The Call

Harriet drove back to Boulder the next morning. She didn't know quite why. She had called Brenda and told her to close the practice until further notice. Her mother would have loved to have her stay longer. She could have just stayed there in Cottonwood Creek.

But her garden would need watering, she told herself. Deeper down, she had the feeling that she needed to be in Boulder if she were ever to unravel the mystery of the Song.

That afternoon, she sat on her little back patio, her elbow on the arm of her folding chair, her brow in her hand. The summer afternoon was warm and soft around her. Dappled leaf shadows fell across her from the sun shining through the young maple that stood in the corner of her pocket-sized backyard.

She had watered and weeded her little garden. There was nothing else for her to do. It was Monday. She should be at work, but everything was changed now. She was empty inside, drained from the intensity of the last weeks, aching with the memory of earth falling on Neal's casket, empty, empty without the Song.

Should I try to call them? she asked herself. The idea that they might actually be extraterrestrials daunted her. Frightened her.

I could move to Cottonwood Creek, she thought. Start my practice there where no one but Winston and Sophie knows about the Song. Just do regular chiropractic like I used to.

She heard a brief scrabbling sound and looked up to see Leah's cat, Tiger, poised on the top of the fence. He swished his tail, then leaped down onto the patio and came to her, purring. "Hi, Tiger," Harriet said.

He rubbed against her legs. She gathered him up into her lap and stroked him. He was warm and solid, rumbling with his purr. His coat was sleek, his green eyes wise and bright. Clearly he was in his prime, a fine, healthy tomcat. Harriet scratched behind his ears, remembering how he had looked and smelled the first time she held him.

"I'm happy to see you looking so well," Harriet told him. He pushed his head against her, asking for deeper scratching.

This is good, Harriet thought. Good that the Song healed him. He's happy, enjoying his life and enriching Leah's. There's really no ambiguity in this case.

She thought of many other healings that had seemed clearly good—Little Jack who, in spite of his collision with the tree, could now have a normal boyhood, Janet who'd had scoliosis and could now stand straight, and Leonard with the broken ankle.

She had run into him—almost literally—a few weeks ago when he came hurtling toward her on his skateboard as she walked up the hill on Broadway. She'd stepped quickly aside, but when he saw her, he leaned back on his board and stopped with dangerous abruptness.

"Hey, Dr. Ellis. How are you?"

Harriet let out the breath she had sucked in when they nearly collided. "I'm fine," she said. "How are you?"

He spread his arms, one foot still on his skateboard. "Look at me. My ankle is perfect, and everything else, too. I've never felt so great in all my life as I have since you sang that wild song to me. That was so awesome."

He was glowing with health, his cheeks flushed, his fair hair tousled, his eyes shining.

"I'm so glad you're doing well," she said.

He sobered. "I'm really grateful, you know. Without what you did, I could've been crippled up for the rest of my life. I'm glad I met you so I could tell you thanks."

He looked into her face for a moment, touched her shoulder. "Take care of yourself now." Then he was off, flying down the hill.

Harriet smiled as she remembered.

Then all the questions and doubts arose again—the Song bouncing back, Mrs. Maloney's warnings, Neal's death.

She jumped up suddenly, spilling Tiger from her lap, crying, "Oh, I don't know. I don't know."

Tiger stalked off, his tail high in indignation.

"Sorry, Tiger," she said. But he was gone, up the maple tree and over the fence.

"I can't just sit here," Harriet said to the tree and the disappearing cat.

She went through her condo, scooped up her purse and walked downtown.

The Boulder mall was alive with street entertainers and musicians, crowds of tourists and shoppers. Harriet glanced around for reporters, but saw no one alarming. In the past, she'd enjoyed going to the mall on weekends, sitting on a bench, and people watching. She slowed down and was heading toward a favorite bench, when a young woman with a baby in a stroller approached her.

"Dr. Ellis!" the young woman exclaimed.

It took a moment for Harriet to recall her name and face. She was Margaret Harris, who had come to her last winter with the baby with leukemia. She was beaming at Harriet, and the baby in the stroller was bright-eyed and chubby cheeked.

"Hello, Margaret. It's good to see you. And this must be Josh." Harriet leaned over and smiled at the baby. He smiled back, a wide grin with new, little white teeth showing.

Harriet felt a rush of joy, seeing him so well. "He looks fine," she said. "What a beautiful little boy."

"He *is* fine. Ever since you healed him, he's been so easy and healthy and happy. Our whole family is better. My husband was so worried when Josh was sick that he lost his job. We were really struggling. He's got a good job now and we're all doing well. Thanks to you. How can we ever thank you enough?"

Harriet noticed that Margaret also looked bright and healthy, quite different from the pale woman in the threadbare coat who had pulled at her sleeve five months ago.

"Just seeing you both so well is all the thanks I need," she said. She bent to touch Josh's plump little hand, and walked on.

She found her bench and sat musing. Healing little Josh was good, she thought. That's clear. Good for the whole family. Her heart lifted as she thought of Josh's bright face and wide smile.

After a while, she got up and wandered farther down the mall. She bought herself an ice cream cone and stopped to listen to a young girl playing Bach on her violin. The child's face was clear and pure, intent on the music. Harriet put several bills in her violin case and strolled on, looking in store windows, watching people. It felt odd to be so idle on a Monday afternoon.

At home, Harriet fixed herself a simple meal and sat out on her patio to eat it. Tiger, having forgiven her for dumping him earlier in the day, came and jumped into her lap. She stroked him absently, her mind going over and over the question of the Song. She remembered Brenda saying bluntly, as was Brenda's way, "If someone doesn't want to be healed, the Song bounces back like it did with your dad and that guy Ron. And if someone's time has come, like your friend Dr. Walker, and you heal him, he dies anyway."

Harriet would give a lot to know what happened to all the old folks the Song had healed at Compassionate Care. She remembered especially Harold Beaner, the little bald man who had hot-wired a car, brought back beer for the celebration, and when last seen, was sauntering out of the nursing home swinging his duffel and chanting, "I'm outta here." Harriet grinned at the memory. Somehow, she guessed, he'd be doing okay.

Set against all her doubts was the unearthly beauty of the Song, the ecstasy of the trance, the wonder of the healing unfolding under her hands, and now seeing some of the results, months later, of that healing.

Finally she stood, lowering Tiger more gently this time, her decision made. "I will call them," she told the cat. She knew how to communicate with them now. Her longing to know them, who they were, and why they had given her the Song overcame all hesitancy. Maybe they could teach her how to use the Song wisely. Was it possible that they would come to her?

Tiger wrapped himself once around her legs, a sleek caress, then jumped onto the fence and disappeared.

She carried her dishes inside but couldn't focus on washing up. She began pacing the length of her little condo. Maybe they *are* the ones who pulled me out of the lake, she thought. If they are extraterrestrials, they might have bodies that could do that.

She shivered in awe. I wonder what they look like. Could I touch them?

The condo was too small for her pacing.

I know, she decided. I'll go up on the ridge where they left me, where we sang the sunrise together. I'll call them from there. Maybe they'll come.

Then she thought, Maybe they'll take me away. Is that what happened before?

Her belly went queasy. Then the strong, stubborn part of her persisted. I have to know. It's been a mystery too long.

She sat on the floor to put on her sandals. Maybe I'd better call Brenda, she thought. Tell her what I'm going to do. In case I'm gone for a while.

She got up and walked to her study, one shoe off and one shoe on.

It took six rings before Brenda answered. She sounded a little breathless.

"Hi, honey," she said. "I was out in the garage tinkering with my Hog. Almost didn't get here in time. How are you doing? Are you home or still in Cottonwood Creek?"

"I'm home. I drove back this morning. Listen, Brenda, I'm going to call them, the bubbles. I'm going to ask them to come to me."

"Atta girl."

"But … I talked with Winston yesterday. He thinks they might be extraterrestrials."

"I thought that, too. Remember? But you wouldn't hear of it."

"I still don't know. But I'm going up on the ridge where they left me and try to call them. If they do come, they might take me away."

"Whoa! You'll come back, won't you?"

"I'm pretty sure I will."

"Are you scared?"

"Yeah."

"Me too. You want me to come with you?"

Harriet had a brief image of Brenda sweating and puffing up the ridge trail, then feared that the Elirians wouldn't come if someone else were with her.

"No. I think I need to do this alone."

"You sure?" A pause on the other end of the line. Harriet could hear Brenda let out a breath. Then she spoke with her usual, reassuring tone. "You'll be all right. Anyone who sings like they do has got to be … maybe they are angels in the form of extraterrestrials. You call me when you get back, hear?"

"I will."

In the gentle summer twilight, the lake was serene, its surface perfectly calm, reflecting the hills above. Harriet walked the familiar trail and came to the ridge path on the far side of the lake. She paused, remembering how she had hidden under the bridge in the snow—long, long ago it seemed. Now water flowed there, smooth and clear under the overhanging willows.

She started up the ridge path. Her mood had changed. Her fear had quieted and now the predominant emotions propelling her up the hill were expectancy, hope, longing.

She climbed, her legs strong, her steps sure. No need to pause to rest, but still she turned partway up to look back at the last glow lingering over the plains, the lights coming on in the city. She passed the hollow where she had sought to end her life. The bushes shielding it were all leafed out, thick and green.

I'm glad the stars called me back, she thought, as she continued her climb, feeling anew the strength and vitality of her body. Even though the ache in her chest for the loss of Neal was still intense, she was glad to be alive.

At the top of the ridge, she found the same flat stone she'd sat on the morning she'd sung the sun up. All around her, tall prairie grass covered the area where she had been bewildered because there had been no footprints in the snow. The evergreen trees standing nearby had new, pale green growth on the tips of their branches. High above her, the waxing half moon sailed white in the evening sky.

Harriet sat down on the rock. She drew in her breath and began to sing. Her voice sounded thin and light. She stopped. It was her old voice, clear and sweet as it had always been, but merely human. Will they hear me if I have only a human voice to sing with? she wondered. It's all I have now. I have to try.

She sang again, letting her small human voice flow out into the twilight, daring to send her prayer on such a fragile thread.

Eliria. Please answer me. I'm sorry I told you to go away. I was frightened. I want to know you, to know who you are. Is it possible for you to come to me? Or can you tell me where I can find you?

She stopped singing. The night was quiet around her. Even the light breeze had stilled.

Then she heard their sweet, unearthly voices singing within her.

We hear you. We see your light on the hill. Wait for us there. We will come to you.

Chapter 28

The Elirians

Harriet pressed her hands against her chest, feeling her heart would break with the blessing of hearing their voices again. How could she ever have sent them away? She watched the light fade over the plains, the stars begin to come out.

And waited.

It seemed a long time, but perhaps it was not so long, for darkness had not fully fallen when she heard their song again, swelling within her, filling all her cells with its beauty and healing. She stood from the flat rock and looked up into the twilit sky.

They drifted down out of the awakening stars, three large spheres glowing softly with a silvery light. Holding her breath, her face tilted up, her arms reaching toward them, Harriet watched, washed in wonder. Slowly, slowly they descended. Then they were around her, floating just above the earth, and she saw that the light that shone from them radiated from their fine, silvery fur. Fur! They were iridescent like the bubbles of her dreams, but they were not bubbles. They were tangible beings covered with fur, except for their wondrous eyes.

Such eyes! Wide set, tilting up at the corners, bottomless, sparkling, light filled, blending all the colors of sky and water.

With a shock, she realized their eyes were like her eyes, the eyes she'd had since her healing. Only they were larger, deeper, unfathomably deep, glowing with wisdom and love.

Out of their mingled song, one familiar voice emerged, rich with overtones, singing, *Harriet, we greet you. We would like to take you to our ship. Will you come with us? We will bring you back safely whenever you wish.*

Harriet was trembling with joy and awe. She started to speak, then remembered to sing, sending her meaning on her song.

Yes. I will go with you.

She turned slowly to look at each one. Their fur was silver yet shimmering with color. One glowed with a rosy color, another was tinged with purple, the third one's fur rippled with pink light.

Arms emerged from their centers, five arms, jointless, fluid, tapering at the ends into many fingered hands. No need for legs. They floated.

They were smiling at her. They had no faces, no mouth to turn up, no nose to wrinkle, no brow to furrow or smooth, only eyes; their eyes smiled.

Never had Harriet even imagined such creatures. Strange, strange they were, yet somehow familiar, evoking inexplicable love in her.

Hesitantly, she reached out and touched the one with rose glow in its fur. Its fur was so soft, so fine, each hair radiant with delicate light.

How? she sang. *How can I go with you? I cannot float as you do.*

We will carry you.

She looked at them in bewilderment. They were about five feet in diameter. Harriet was six feet tall. *But I am so big.*

Laughter rippled in their song. Another, deeper voice sang, *It is far easier to take you up from here than to pull you out of the bottom of the lake.*

"Oh!" Harriet exclaimed, forgetting to sing. She stared at the three round beings, her mouth open, her eyes wide. All the pieces fell into place, like a kaleidoscope shifting into pattern. It was they who had rescued her, healed her, and brought her back to where she now stood— drifting down, lingering to sing with her, never touching Earth. That was why there had been no foot prints.

Strong arms came around her. Harriet startled. The purple-tinged being gathered her up with its five arms, folded her into a fetal position, and cradled her into its exquisitely fine fur. She felt the slow, strong beating of a heart against her cheek. Slowly, they floated upward, the other two beings floating beside them, their song swelling in its beauty and power.

Memory flooded back. She had been carried this way before. In this way she had returned from icy death to this silken fur, this warm embrace, this beating heart. She remembered the hands on her shoulders, drawing her up through the ice, the strong arms enfolding her.

She felt her body soften, then let go completely into the embrace and the sure knowledge that she was safe and loved.

Only for a short time they floated upward. Harriet felt them hover, then move horizontally. She lifted her head and saw that they were now in an enclosed space, a circular room with big arched windows all around.

It was the same room she had found herself in when she sent the Song away and watched the windows darken one by one. Now, though it was night outside, starlight shone through. And inside, there was soft light circulating in rainbow colors. She breathed it in and remembered more, remembered breathing that rainbow light as she lay slowly returning to consciousness.

Gently, the being who had carried her set her on her feet. Two more spheres floated toward her, one with deep green eyes the color of Harriet's and fur tinged with gold, and another iridescent with shades of blue.

She remembered. She remembered these five beautiful beings, remembered that she had known them, known their names, their eyes, their voices, and had loved them. How could she have forgotten? And she also knew there was much more that she still did not remember.

Harriet was suddenly dizzy. The room seemed to spin. She sank to her knees and laid her brow on the floor. The floor, too, she remembered. Unlike any substance of Earth, it was warm and soft and of such delicate resilience that it felt like resting on a gossamer spider web.

The five beings gathered around her. A gentle hand smoothed her head. Other hands touched her body. She felt their healing light pouring into her, and that, too, she remembered.

She sat up on her heels and sang to them. *I forgot. I forgot all of you. I forgot this place where you healed me.*

Then she bent her head again, ashamed. *I'm sorry. I don't know why I forgot. It was ungrateful of me when you healed me and brought me back from death and gave me the Song. And I still don't remember why or all that you taught me.*

Ah! Their song of compassion washed over her. *Do not be ashamed. We have rescued many Earthlings, brought them here and healed them, and only one remembered. All the others, if they retained anything, thought they had dreamed. It is hard for minds of Earth to know us. Rest now. We will help you remember.*

They sat close around her, touching her with their wise, seven-fingered hands. Breathing in the rainbow light with its ineffable fragrance, Harriet closed her eyes as the memories unfolded.

First came the shocking memory of drowning: She was struggling, gripped in panic. This was it. Her last breath gone, her lungs filling with frigid, black water. She had stopped flailing, gone limp, and was slowly sinking when she heard singing within her, song like nothing she had ever heard before. Many voices sang, each voice a little different, unearthly harmony, like the music of the spheres, stars dancing their vast circles in the depths of the universe. Hands gripped her shoulders. One last wisp of thought slipped through her. *They are taking me to heaven.*

Harriet's eyes flew open. She was trembling. There was a reason she hadn't remembered that before. It was too terrifying. Only now, enfolded in the love of the furry beings surrounding her, could she dare to remember.

Ah, they sang. *You are safe now.*

Harriet took a long, deep breath. Rainbow light filled her, renewed her.

This light— Harriet gestured at the rainbow colors circling around them. *When I breathe, it … heals me.*

It is essence of Eliria, the rose colored being sang. *It is our nourishment. We cannot live long without it. We do not eat or have to kill other life to live as you do. We take in the essence of our planet through our fur. A reservoir of it is built into our ship, a supply to last us a year.*

Then more memories came flooding back, perhaps because she was breathing Elirian light. Harriet looked again at the beings surrounding her and no longer saw strange creatures, but familiar beloveds. Recognition, then joy and heart-bursting love rushed through her. Tears sprang to her eyes. She felt as if her whole body was smiling.

I remember you now, she sang. She touched the one whose fur was iridescent with purple and sang her name. *Merilea, you are the one who carried me that first night.*

Harriet also remembered that they were neither male nor female, but that she had thought of them as female because of their sensitive touch and their soft, furry bodies.

Merilea was slightly larger than the others. Her eyes were gray with traces of purple, like water flowing in the shadow of a cliff. *Yes,* she sang in her deep voice. She touched a hand to her heart and then to Harriet's heart.

Harriet turned to the one whose fur glowed with rose light. *And you are Kiria.* Kiria's eyes were deep blue, green, gray, shot with light like the sun shining into the depths of the ocean. She touched her heart and then touched Harriet's heart and sang, *Yes.*

Turning slowly Harriet greeted each one, looking into their eyes, speaking their names. Rosiri was the blue tinted one whose sapphire eyes sparkled like the sun on a wind-rippled lake. Lillilia had pale pink light in her fur, and her eyes were soft blue-gray with wisps of pink like the sky at dawn. Tirini with the gold-tinted fur was the one with deep green eyes the color of Harriet's. Each one touched her hand to her heart and then to Harriet's heart.

Harriet now remembered this ritual of greeting, hand to heart to heart. In this way they had introduced themselves to her the morning after her rescue, as she lay on the soft, warm floor of the circular room, breathing rainbow light and realizing that nothing, nothing in all her body hurt.

She had awakened from a long dream of their singing, their hands moving over her. At first she had been frightened. Then she had turned to see Merilea sitting beside her.

"Who, what are you?" she had stammered.

Then they had all come, touched their hearts and sang their names within her.

Harriet sat silent, remembering, looking from one to another, wishing she had as many hands as they did so she could hold hands with all of them.

I called you again and again, she sang, *wanting to know who you were. Tirini, Kiria, you gave me your names in my dreams, but I didn't know they were names. And you gave me the word Eliria. Is that the name of your planet?*

They sang then of Eliria, their voices blending, their song soaring with the beauty of their faraway home. Harriet received images of a verdant planet, with lakes and streams flowing amidst strange, rich vegetation, tall trees like none of Earth, and flowers, also strange to Harriet, but breathtaking in their vivid colors. Silvery, iridescent spheres floated among them. Rainbow light circled the planet. Harriet seemed to see the image shimmering through light years of stars.

Why have you come so far? she asked.

We have come to study humankind, they sang. *The dissonance on Planet Earth has become so severe that it is distorting the balance of the web.*

The web? Harriet asked.

Kiria sang then. *The universe is held together by an energetic web. All the stars, moons, planets are connected by the fine lines of the web.* As she sang, she gestured with her fluid arms and many-fingered hands, and Harriet received the image of a vast gossamer web moving in spirals, stars, moons, and planets scattered throughout. Kiria's song deepened.

The web holds us all in balance. There are many intelligent life forms inhabiting the planets scattered among the stars. They have learned to communicate and travel on the lines of the web and have formed a council to promote the harmony of the universe. We are all gravely concerned about the dissonance coming from Planet Earth. We have sent emissaries over the millennia to show another way, to share the light, but many have been killed by the Earthlings, some have been lost, and only a few returned to the council.

Harriet felt a wave of grief as she thought of all the suffering and violence she read about each day in the paper. *I know well of the dissonance,* she sang. *But what can you do?*

Tirini picked up the song with her bell-like voice. *Each race has its own gifts. Ours is healing through song and seeing into the essence of things. We have come in five ships, each one to study a different part of your planet. Our ship is studying the part you call North America. We have been here almost a year of your time and studied many humans. The emissaries have not failed. As we circle your planet, we can see those they have touched, like points of light in the darkness.* Tirini, too, danced with her arms as she sang, and Harriet saw the ships hovering over the continents, the points of light in the darkness. *But,* Tirini sang, *the emissaries who were able to return to the council say that it is very difficult for Earthlings to hold the light. They forget and become entangled in the discord. We have come to learn more of human essence in the hopes that the next emissaries can be more successful in helping you humans free yourselves of the dissonance.*

Despair closed down on Harriet. *The dissonance is so big, so awful, so ingrained. All the violence and hatred. It seems impossible to do anything to change it.*

Lillilia's high, sweet voice answered, *Each act of kindness, even the smallest one, makes a difference.*

Rosiri sang in a minor key in her strange, haunting voice. *We did not know of pain or death until we came here. We grieve for you. Life is difficult on Planet Earth.*

Harriet still held the image of Eliria and remembered the message she had received under the ponderosas, that there was no pain on Eliria. *What a blessed life you lead,* she sang. *No pain! Do you die?*

No, they sang together. *We are of Eliria. We rise out of her when we are called by an ulada, sink in again when our ulada is complete.*

Ulada? Harriet asked.

An ulada is a mission we are called to, Lillilia sang, *to create more harmony on our planet or in the universe. It can be a simple thing, like singing to a new tree until it is strong, or it can be huge, like the ulada that called us here.*

And when you are called, Harriet asked, *do you know what your ulada is?*

Oh, yes, they all sang. *Knowing is what calls us.*

Oh! Harriet exclaimed. *How different our world would be if we knew we were called to create harmony, given a clear mission! Most of us spend our whole lives wondering what we are here for, and creating a lot of chaos as we try to figure it out.*

They sat in silence for a while. Harriet pondered the idea of an ulada. Did she have an ulada? Then all the doubts and fears of the last weeks, all the searching of the last months rose into one passionate question.

Breaking the gentle silence, she blurted, *Why did you give me the Song?*

Ah, they sang, *when we saw how much suffering there was on Planet Earth, we wanted to leave something for you. We cannot stay. Our ulada is to be here only a year, to study humankind, and bring back what we learn to the council. But we thought that if we could leave the Song behind with a few of you, you could ease some of the suffering.*

Harriet bent her head, her heart aching for her torn world. She gripped tighter the hands she held. Other hands stroked and soothed her.

Then the question that had tormented her the most arose. *But why did you choose me?*

Because of your light, Kiria sang. *Every being on this Earth has a light, but for most the light is dim. For some it can hardly be seen at all. We saw your light. It was bright and clear in spite of the pain you carried. We watched how you cared for your patients. We were waiting for an opportunity to come to you.*

Tirini chimed in in her bell-like voice. *The night you fell through the ice, we were far to the south, returning a child who had been injured, But Rosiri was watching over you and called us to come quickly.*

We almost lost you, Merilea sang.

Harriet felt her heart beating, her breath rising and falling, life flowing through her. *Thank you,* she sang almost in a whisper. *Thank you for saving me. Thank you for healing me.*

We were sad when you told us to take the Song back, Rosiri sang. *We are glad that you called to us, and that you are here with us now.*

You are not the only one to whom the Song has been given, Kiria sang. *Those of us in the other four spaceships around your planet have given the Song to a few humans. But only a few. It is hard to find those who can carry the power of it without misusing it. You are one of those rare few.*

They sat silently together again. Harriet felt a swelling in her heart, like a bud pressing against its calyx, the beginning of something opening. She breathed deep of the rainbow air, drank in the healing of the Elirians' touch.

You have other questions, Kiria sang. *We can feel them agitating your heart.*

Harriet could feel her heart agitating, too. Her next questions tumbled out in a burst of song. *But what about when the Song bounces back?* she asked. *What about someone whose time has come?* She hesitated. *Like Neal.*

If the Song bounces back, it is not their ulada to be healed at that time, Kiria answered. *And if their time has come, it means that their ulada is complete. Then the Song can ease their suffering but will not keep them from dying.*

Only with Neal, Merilea sang, *his ulada was not quite complete when you sang to him. There was one more piece that he completed on his last day.* Her eyes smiled. *You will see.*

Harriet was stilled with wonder. They made it sound so simple and clear. She looked around at them, meeting their deep eyes, feeling their love. The swelling in her heart increased.

Are you angels? she asked.

Angels? They sang the word back and forth, their song rising in question, asking each other, reaching into her to understand the meaning behind her word.

Messengers of God, she explained.

God? Again their song weaved and rose in question.

Then they sang together, *You mean the Oneness.*

Their voices blended in harmony, sweeter, fuller, deeper than ever she had heard them sing before. They continued singing. Their song was a hymn of love and beauty beyond the heart's deepest longing.

Harriet wept. How could she ever have doubted? She felt herself dissolved into an ocean of light as the hymn sang within her and all around her, flowing out from the spaceship into all the universe.

Even when the hymn ended and silence enfolded them again, Harriet still felt the immensity of their Song echoing through her, transforming her in some way she couldn't yet comprehend. She pressed her hands to her cheeks, wiping away her tears.

Then Kiria sang alone. *We are all of the Oneness, every star, every planet, all life forms on all the planets. We are all of the Oneness, just as we Elirians are of Eliria, rising from her and returning to her.*

We have learned as we study you humans, Rosiri sang in her strange, haunting voice, *that you fear death, and that your fear of death lies behind the dissonance of your planet. Fear does terrible things to you—sickness, violence, cruelty. But there is no need to fear. We all return to the Oneness and arise again from the Oneness. There is no separation, no death. Only the ending of one ulada and the beginning of another.*

The Song also arises from the Oneness, Kiria sang. *When you sing and heal with it, you and the one you touch remember that you, too, are part of the Oneness.*

Harriet nodded. *When I heal with the Song, I do feel part of the Oneness. It is the deepest happiness I know.*

Your happiness shifts the web, Merilea sang. *As does the happiness of those you heal. Even the cat,* she added, a ripple of laughter in her song.

Harriet smiled, remembering the purring warmth of Tiger in her lap only a few hours earlier. Barely daring, she asked, *Is it my ulada then, to heal with the Song?*

We believe it is, Kiria sang.

They were silent again. Harriet felt the pressure in her heart swelling almost unbearably. Was it truly her ulada to heal with the Song? She remembered the first day Neal had given her an adjustment, and her resolution to follow in his footsteps, to help those in pain. She had never wavered from that goal.

Do not fear, Rosiri sang. *You need only to give the Song wherever it will be received. All will be well.*

With a soft burst, the pressure in Harriet's chest released. A white rose bloomed in her heart, its fragrance filling all her being. Her path was clear. She took a deep breath. *Will you give me the Song again?*

They all sang then, a rush of gladness. *We will.*

They gathered closer around her. Each one placed a hand on her heart as they linked their other hands in an intricate pattern that enclosed her. Softly they began to sing, then their song deepened. Enriched by their wondrous voices, Harriet heard the themes and melodies that she had sung over the last months as the Song healed through her. Then she was singing with them, the Song pouring through her and beyond her, out into the stars, drifting down to bless the Earth.

Chapter 29

Return

*H*arriet walked slowly down the ridge path, the Elirians' farewell song still resonating within her. It was mid-morning. The summer sun was hot. Below her, the lake lay like a blue jewel in the midst of green prairie grass and trees. As she descended, the distant sound of traffic and the low roar of the city floated up to her.

The farther down she walked into her everyday world, the more her night with the Elirians seemed like a dream. Parts of it were already beginning to slip away.

She stopped. Panic rushed through her. "No!" she exclaimed aloud. "I must not forget again."

She began to run, down the steep slope, pebbles scattering from under her feet. She ran, repeating under her breath, "No, no. I mustn't forget," all the way to her car. She drove home recklessly fast and burst into her condo.

Throwing down her sweatshirt, kicking off her shoes, she ran to her computer.

I must write it down, all of it, she thought desperately. *Please*, she sent her prayer to the Elirians, *help me remember.*

Their song filled her. *We are with you. We will help you.*

Harriet let out a sob of relief. *Thank you.*

Her hands were sweaty. She rubbed them on her jeans, took a deep breath, opened a new document, and began to write.

Hours later, she pushed back her chair and stood. Her back was tired from hunching over the computer so long and she was hungry, but she felt at peace. It was all written down, and she'd even put a copy in Dropbox in case her computer crashed.

She went to her kitchen and put together a cheese sandwich, poured herself some lemonade, and took them out to the table on her patio. She realized she hadn't eaten since the evening before and it was mid-afternoon now. But I wasn't hungry with the Elirians, she thought, because I was breathing their rainbow air.

Then the wonder of them swept through her again. Her sandwich lay half-eaten on her plate as she leaned her head on her hand and drifted into memories of the night before.

Once she had received the Song again, they had sung together a long time, the Song of healing blending into the hymn of The Oneness. Tears slid between Harriet's fingers, as she felt again the ecstasy, the ineffable wonder of that hymn that had seemed to flow into every cell of her body and at the same time reach to the farthest star. She remembered the sensation of it winding around her heart, dissolving the bitter, sharp shards of her grief …

"Oh!" Harriet lifted her head and sat up straight. She put her hand over her heart. There was still a deep ache there like the scar of an old wound, but the piercing anguish was gone! She took a deep breath. It moved freely through her chest. She thought of Neal, saw his face smiling at her with infinite tenderness, and was washed in love and gratitude, realizing that all they'd shared was part of the wholeness, the joy and sorrow of being incarnate.

Can the Song heal even that? she marveled. At the same moment, she understood how it had happened and how she could guide the Song to ease the grief of others.

Then the experience of dissolving in the ocean of light immersed her again. She touched her heart, smoothed her cheek—as Neal had done that last time they were together. Everything in her little garden was sparkling, vivid, and clear in a way she had never seen before. Never such blue in the sky, such infinite green in the leaves of the trees. Each blade of grass seemed lit from below. She went to the young maple and leaned her brow against its trunk for a long time, feeling the pulse of its life and that it was one with the pulse of her life.

Finally she returned to the table. The vividness had faded slightly. But I have seen it, she thought. I know now what my garden really looks like, full of the light of The Oneness.

She took a few bites of her sandwich, laid it down, and drifted again.

I never did ask about my eyes. They said I could ask them anything, anytime as long as they are here. But they'll only be here a little longer.

Rosiri had told her they would be returning to the intergalactic council on the last day of August. Harriet had asked if she would still be able to communicate with them after they left Earth, and Rosiri had answered sadly, *No, it is too far.*

Only a little more than six weeks and then they would be gone.

But I have touched them, she thought. I have sung with them. I have spent the night nestled in their shining fur, enfolded in their many arms, and now I know what my ulada is. I will be faithful to it as long as I live.

She picked up her sandwich again. If Brenda were here, she'd tell me to eat, she thought with a smile. Oh, I promised to call her. What can I possibly say?

She realized she was in a seriously altered state.

She finished her sandwich and went to her study. The phone seemed like a strange and foreign thing.

Brenda answered on the first ring. "Harriet, am I glad to hear from you! I hardly slept a wink last night wondering where you were and what was happening. Are you okay?"

Harriet almost started to sing her answer. She hesitated, seeking the appropriate voice for Brenda. Finally she answered, "I'm okay."

"What happened?"

"They came. They took me up to their spaceship."

"Whoa!" There was a long silence. "Then they *are* extraterrestrials?"

"Yes, and they're also angels, but not like the pictures with blond curly hair and harps."

Brenda snorted. "I never did think angels looked like that. It's a Caucasian projection. But what *did* they look like?"

Harriet didn't know how to answer. She saw them again—their eyes, their round bodies with iridescent fur, their five fluid arms, their many-fingered hands.

"I … I don't know how to tell you. They are not like anything you could imagine. They're round and iridescent like the bubbles in my dreams, but they're not bubbles. They're … physical. You can touch them. They're covered with fur."

"Fur! Like animals?"

"No, not like any earthly thing. But they're beautiful. They have the most amazing eyes." Tears rose as Harriet felt her love of them. "They are the ones who rescued me. They float. That's why there were no footprints."

"Nooo kidding! Are you sure you're all right? You sound kinda funny."

"I'm fine, just a bit spaced out. It's a little hard to talk. I spent the night sleeping in their arms. And they gave me back the Song."

Harriet heard Brenda's sigh of relief. "That's great. Are you okay to use it now?"

"Yes."

"Can I schedule tomorrow?"

Harriet did an inner check. She still felt strange and light, as if barely embodied, but somehow knew that tomorrow she'd be okay to sing the Song again. "Yes, I can come tomorrow."

"Whew. I'd better get on the phone. There's a pile of folks lined up. You rest, honey. I can't wait to see you tomorrow."

⇐ ⇒

When Harriet arrived at the office the next morning, Brenda wrapped her in a fierce hug. "Honey, I'm so glad to see you." She held Harriet out at arm's length and looked her up and down. "There. You look like yourself again. Only even shinier. Did those angels put a bunch of light bulbs inside you?"

Harriet smiled. "Not exactly." She returned Brenda's hug, filled with love and gratitude for her faithful friend.

At lunch, Brenda wanted to know all about her time with the Elirians. Harriet told her what she could, but it was hard to find words for the deeper shifts within her. It was okay. Brenda was thrilled with the descriptions of the Elirians and their ship, and with the most important fact that Harriet had received the Song again.

The rhythm of that first day back was the same as before Neal's death. The Song moved through her hands, the healings unfolded, patients came and went. But the feel of the day was profoundly different. The weight of her doubts and fears was gone. She hadn't realized how much it had burdened her. The ecstasy of the trance, without that burden, was purer than ever before. She still felt light, almost disembodied, but most of all clear, clear this was her path.

Chapter 30

Inheritance

Friday evening, Harriet set out for Cottonwood Creek. She knew Sophie was there checking in on their mother, but Harriet wanted to be there, too, to sing to her mother and be sure no new physical difficulties had come up. Her mother had seemed okay the previous weekend, managing well, but Harriet didn't know how she really was responding to her husband's death.

She also realized as she drove how much she wanted to see Winston. She couldn't wait to share with him all that had happened. She knew he would understand the thoughts and feelings that had been hard to explain to Brenda.

She arrived just at dusk. The evenings were still long so soon after summer solstice, pink clouds drifting over the faraway peaks to the west.

Her mother greeted her warmly. "Honey, I'm so glad to see you. I'm doing okay, but it does feel strange, rattling around in this big house all by myself. Your room's all ready for you. You go on up and get settled. I've made a chicken pot pie for dinner."

Harriet had been so distressed over Neal's death the weekend before that she hadn't looked around much. Upstairs, she peeked into her parents' bedroom, and saw a new bedspread, with pink roses, on the bed. Her father had liked plain colors only. The dark blue curtains were still the same, but Harriet suspected they, too, would soon be changed.

The house did feel emptier. Harriet realized what a presence her father had been. In the living room, the TV was turned off and covered with a white cloth. In place of his old chair by the stove was a new one, comfy and upholstered in a blue floral pattern with a padded matching footstool.

"Sophie bought it for me up in Parker," her mother explained. "Harry liked sitting by the stove so much. I think I will like it when the weather gets cold again."

When it was bedtime, Harriet lay down with her mother and sang to her. There was nothing serious amiss, but the Song touched up a few small issues.

If I keep doing this, Harriet thought as she crossed the hall to her room, she may live forever. Would she want that? Doubt arose, but then she remembered Rosiri's sparkling, deep blue eyes and her odd, haunting voice singing, *Do not fear. You need only to give the Song wherever it will be received.* And Kiria singing that the Song could ease the suffering of the dying, but would not hold them to life when their ulada was complete.

❧ ❧

The next morning after the breakfast dishes were washed, Harriet wanted to see Winston. I could just walk over to the manse and knock on his door, she thought. But she felt hesitant. Maybe she should call first. While she was wavering, the phone rang.

"Harriet?" It was a man's voice, not Winston's.

"Yes."

"This is Roger, Roger Walker. I heard you were in town."

How in the world did he hear? Harriet wondered. She'd only arrived the night before. Maybe someone had seen her car in the driveway. She shook her head. The small-town news circuit was alive and well.

"Hi, Roger," she said. "What's up?"

"I'd like to stop over if I may. I need to talk with you. Is this morning okay?"

Harriet's eyes widened. Roger, Neal's son. What would he want to talk about? A streak of panic ran through her. Did he know? She swallowed. "Sure. This morning's fine. Come on over."

Fifteen minutes later, the doorbell rang. Roger was neatly dressed in jeans and a green T-shirt, his light brown hair combed back, a briefcase in his hand. Seeing the briefcase, Harriet remembered that Roger was the town lawyer.

They settled in the living room.

"I've got some big news for you," Roger said. "I've been going over my dad's will. He left you that little house that used to be his office."

Harriet's jaw dropped. The little yellow house with the peeling paint …

"Oh, my goodness," she said.

"He came to me the morning before he died—" Roger stopped speaking, his jaw clenched. He brought a fist up toward his chest. "I could kill that fool kid who ran over him. Dad was so much better." He stopped speaking again, and took a deep breath. "Sorry, it hit us all so hard. What I'm wanting to tell you—he came to me that morning, said he wanted to open his practice again, he'd talked with you and you were going to come down and join him, so he didn't have to work full time. He looked so good and happy, better than he had in years. It was some kind of miracle. He wanted me to change his will so you would get the office if anything happened to him."

Roger's voice broke in a half sob. "We didn't dream something would happen that very day. Sorry," he said again, pulling himself together. "It's just that … we'd accepted that he was dying, but then when he got better …"

Harriet's heart ached at the rawness of his grief. She wanted to touch him, and let the Song ease his grief as it had hers, but something told her the time was not right.

"Anyway," Roger said, "that little house is yours. It's a bit run down. Dad didn't seem to notice; he was just used to things being as they'd always been. Then he collapsed one day and never went back. So it needs some attention, but it's still set up to be an office. I was talking to Nan and some other folks. We're hoping that, even though Dad's gone, you'll still come down and practice here. There's need. Do you think you will?"

Harriet was silent, remembering Merilea singing, *Neal's ulada was not quite complete when you sang to him. There was one more piece that he completed on his last day. You will see.*

Her mind spun. So it was Neal's ulada, the very last piece of it, to open the space for her to come to Cottonwood Creek to carry on his practice.

"I don't know," she said finally. "I was planning to, then got thrown off by your dad's death. But it seems this gift of the house is a pretty strong message."

Roger smiled then. "Looks that way to me. You'd be welcome. Folks here think a lot of you."

"I'll have to think about it," she said. "It would be a big change for me."

Roger stood. "Keep me posted. If there is anything I can do for you, let me know. Oh." He reached into his pants pocket. "Here's the key. I'll get the paperwork and title to you soon."

Harriet saw him to the door, then dropped onto the couch, gazing in stunned amazement at the key in her hand.

Harriet's mother had been in the kitchen while Harriet and Roger talked. Harriet had subliminally noticed that cooking sounds had stopped sometime during their conversation.

Now her mother hurried into the living room. "I couldn't help hearing," she said. "Are you really going to come back home to do your chiropractic here in Cottonwood Creek? Honey, I'd love that. You can live right here with me."

Harriet stood up to hug her mother, smothering a chuckle over the couldn't-help-hearing bit. "I'm not sure yet, Mom. But thanks for the offer to stay with you. That would make my transition easier." She held her mother close, then bent to kiss her cheek.

"I need to go see Reverend Harvey," she said. "I want to talk it over with him. I'll be back for lunch."

Her hesitancy about seeing Winston was gone. She waved good-bye to her mother, stepped out the side door, and took off at a fast walk.

A stout elderly man was mowing his lawn across the street from the manse. He shut down the mower when he saw Harriet. "Hi, there, Harrie," he called.

"Hi, Mr. Hopkins."

"How's your mom doing? It's a hard thing when your life partner passes away."

Harriet didn't quite stop. She was intent on seeing Winston. She slowed enough to answer. "She's doing okay. She's a strong woman, and Sophie and I are both watching over her."

"You tell her hello for me." Mr. Hopkins hitched up his suspenders. "Tell her if she needs anything to let me know."

"Thanks, Mr. Hopkins. I'll tell her."

She was halfway across the street when Mr. Hopkins called, "You looking for the preacher? He's not there. The wife saw him heading to the church an hour ago."

"Okay." Harriet waved and changed direction. The church was next door to the manse, separated only by the parking lot and the lawn. Harriet went around to the side door and stopped at the foot of the stairs leading up to Winston's office. Her heart was racing with the intensity of all she wanted to share with him. Calm down, she admonished herself. She took a big breath and went up. Her footsteps echoed on the wood floor of the upstairs hall.

The door to Winston's office was open. He was sitting at his desk, writing. Harriet knocked lightly on the door frame.

"Harriet!" He pushed back his chair and came to her.

His smile was so warm and welcoming and Harriet was so glad to see him that she almost hugged him. She caught her breath and blushed.

He took both her hands in his. "I was hoping you'd come down this weekend. I've been thinking of you all week." He paused, studying her face. "How are you? You look much better. Like yourself again."

"I *am* better." She hesitated. "I know it's Saturday and you have a lot to prepare for tomorrow, but if you have time … I'd love to talk with you."

"I've plenty of time. Come, sit down." He led her to the couch and pulled up a chair to sit opposite her. "How has your week been?"

The answer to that question was so big, that at first Harriet couldn't speak at all. Finally, she blurted "Huge!"

"Huge? Tell me."

"I met the Elirians."

Winston straightened in his chair. "You *met* them?"

"Yes." Harriet suddenly felt herself smiling all over her body with the joy and excitement of what she had to share. "And they are beautiful, beautiful beyond words."

Winston's eyes widened. "Tell me," he said again.

So Harriet poured out her story—her decision to call the Elirians, the way they floated down to her out of the evening sky, their voices, their eyes, their spaceship, the story of how they had come to study humans, and their concern for the disharmony of planet Earth.

She could tell Winston about the hymn of the Oneness, the rose that had opened in her heart, and her ulada. And she knew that, even though he was lost in amazement, he understood.

Tears came to his eyes as she described receiving the Song again and singing with the Elirians the hymn of the Oneness out into the stars and down to bless the Earth. "You look beautiful," he said. "I can see the rose blooming in your heart."

Harriet didn't know what to say to that. She changed the subject. "There's more," she said.

"More news?"

"Yes. Just this morning, Roger Walker came over to tell me that Neal willed me the little house that used to be his office. Roger said that he and Nan, and some other folks he's talked to, hope that I'll come down and open a practice here. I was planning, as I told you last week, to come work with Neal. Then when he died … It seems changing the will was one of the last things he did. I wanted to talk with you about it. I'm thinking I might like to come back. To a smaller town, closer to family."

A wide smile had been spreading across Winston's face as Harriet spoke. Now he burst out, "Harriet, you really might? That would be— I'd be so happy to have you living here in town, not just coming down on weekends. The church, the whole community would be enhanced. I'd—" He stopped, his cheeks flushed. He looked away for a moment, pulled a pen out of his shirt pocket, and turned it in his hands.

Harriet's insides were tumbling. There was no mistaking the energy pouring out from Winston, his smile, the light in his eyes. She felt a responding energy rising up in her, flowing back to him. She bent her head, hiding her face behind her hair. Inside her an amazed little voice whispered, He's in love with me! I didn't know he felt that way … I didn't know I did.

Hush, she told it.

She glanced up at him. He was looking at her again.

"Wait a minute," he said laughing, still blushing. "I should be asking you how you feel, not telling you how I feel. That's not very ministerial."

Harriet was blushing, too. "You don't have to be ministerial with me." She shifted to one hip and reached into her jeans' pocket. "I have the key," she said, opening her palm to show him.

"To the office? Have you been over there yet?"

"I haven't been inside since Neal sent me away when I was twenty-three. I did stop by and look at it from the outside last winter, when I knew Neal wasn't there anymore. It's kind of rundown."

"Let's go look at it." He hesitated, his cheeks flushed again. "I mean, would you like me to go with you?"

"I would." Harriet felt a bubble of excitement rising in her. "Now?"

"Why not?" Winston stood. "Where is it?"

"Not far." Harriet got up and tucked the key back into her pocket. "It's on Second Street, just a few blocks from the creek."

Winston took her arm. "Let's go."

As they came out of the church, Harriet saw that Mr. Hopkins had finished mowing the lawn and was relaxing in his porch swing. He waved as they passed. They waved back.

"I'd forgotten," Harriet said, as they started walking. "You didn't come to Cottonwood Creek until after Neal had closed his practice and gone to California. Did you ever meet him?"

"Just once. I called on him when he came home, just a few days before your dad died. Then everything got busy and I never saw him alive again. He seemed a fine man."

"He was."

"How are you doing with your grieving?"

Harriet stopped walking and turned to look into his face.

"Much better. It all shifted when I was with the Elirians. Sometime in our singing, my heart was eased. I still miss Neal, I'll always love him, but losing him is not so sharp and desperate as it was. I'm seeing a bigger picture now, just being so grateful for all the love and joy we shared, for all he taught me. I know now that even sadness is part of the Oneness."

"You've gained wisdom from all your sorrow. That's a big shift."

"It is. I'm still integrating it."

They walked again. Harriet repressed an impulse to slip her hand into his.

When they reached the little yellow house, Harriet saw that the paint was peeling even more than when she'd seen it the winter before. The lawn was brown and dry, uncut, full of stalky weeds. The flower gardens along the walk were dead.

"It's been neglected since Neal got sick," she said. "It used to be really pretty."

"It can be again," Winston said. "Shall we go in?"

Harriet went ahead of him. Her knees were shaky, her belly queasy. She had the odd sense that she was once again the awkward sixteen-year-old going up the walk for the first time. What would it be like to go through that door again?

The hinges creaked as she swung it open. As she stepped into the waiting room, a vortex of memories swirled around her. She put her hand on the edge of the desk to steady herself. She could feel Winston behind her.

"Give me a minute," she said. "This place is packed with memories."

"It's okay. Take your time." He stepped back and waited quietly by the door.

She looked around, took a few steps into the waiting room. The same beige couch and green upholstered chairs were still there. After thirty years? she marveled. The couch sagged, the chairs were faded and worn. The potted plant on the coffee table was dead. On the other side of the desk, the office she'd kept as a teenager was little changed. The same telephone, the same bookcases and file cabinets. Only the typewriter was gone, replaced by a computer.

The carpet was also faded and worn. The center of the hall that led to the treatment room was threadbare. Harriet remembered how many times a day Neal had walked up and down that hall, seeing one patient out and greeting the next.

Winston was looking around, too. Harriet turned to him. "This room used to be bright and cozy. It looks so shabby now."

"That's nothing that a fresh coat of paint and new carpet wouldn't fix. New furniture, too. Everything else looks basically sound. It still has a cozy feel." He gestured to the hall. "What's down this way?"

"The treatment room."

Harriet led the way. The door was open. Harriet went to the treatment table, laid her hand on it, and stroked the surface. It was on this same table that she and Neal had made love almost daily that last summer before she went to college. She remembered as if it were yesterday the sweetness of his skin, the taste of him.

"I had my first chiropractic adjustment on this table," she told Winston. "This very same table. It's strange he never got a new one, They've had electric ones for decades, ones that go up and down and make your work much easier."

"He was probably so used to this one he didn't want a new one."

"That would be like him." Harriet turned slowly around, gazing at the familiar room. There was the small desk where he had sat to write his notes, the chair for the patient, the wheeled stool, also quite worn. The window looking out onto the back lawn and the cottonwood tree, the shelves with supplements, probably all out of date by now. All, all the same.

"Roger said Neal never came back after the day he got sick," she said. "There's still laundry in the basket here. And the dead plant on the coffee table in the waiting room."

Suddenly, it all felt too much. The ache in her chest was threatening to dissolve into tears. "Let's go now," she said. "I've seen enough to get an idea."

She moved quickly down the hall, through the waiting room, Winston following her, and didn't stop until she'd locked the door and was standing on the street in front of the house.

"Kind of intense to see it all again?" Winston asked.

"Yeah."

"Shall we go sit by the creek a little while? I know you wanted to talk over your decision about moving here. I can be ministerial now."

Harriet smiled at that. "Okay. That sounds good."

They started walking the two blocks to the creek. "How is it feeling now that you've seen the house?" Winston asked.

"A little overwhelming. All the memories. You're right. Some fixing up would make a big difference. I guess what's more overwhelming is the thought of following in Neal's footsteps. He was so skilled, such an important part of this town for so many years. So loved."

"As you would be. As you are already, and not just because of your singing in church. I'm remembering your birthday party, how people were celebrating you. And you would be bringing the Song with all its healing. Would you miss Boulder?"

"Yes. Some things. I love having the mountains near, walking around the lake. Before I received the Song, I would have missed my clients, but now I don't see the same ones three times a week as I used to. They come once, the Song heals them, and then they don't need me again. So I'm always seeing new people. I'm booked way ahead. I could tell Brenda not to take any new clients, but still it would be a couple of months before I could finish with all those already scheduled. I'm pretty sure Brenda would come with me. She said she would when we were thinking of coming down to work with Neal. I'd have a hard time doing without Brenda." Harriet sighed and rubbed her brow. "All that would need to be done—close the practice, move my home—is pretty daunting."

They had reached the creek. A little way down the path were some rocks by the water where they had often sat to converse. When they were settled there, Winston said, "Imagine that all the transition has been handled and you are living here, the little house all fixed up, Brenda with you, your practice established, how would that feel?"

Harriet closed her eyes. She listened to the song of the creek, breathed in the hot, dry air of Colorado summer, the smell of grass and earth and water. She let images flow of practicing in the little house, living again in a small town where everyone knows everyone—and everyone's business. Being close to her mother and Sophie and Mary and the little ones.

"It feels good," she said at last. "I would miss some things about Boulder, but there's a lot I'd be glad to leave behind. It's peaceful here. I wouldn't have the mountains near, but I'd have this creek. And everyone who knows of the possibility of my moving here has been so welcoming—Roger and Nan, my mother … you.

She dared to turn her head and look at him. He met her eyes. "I would truly welcome you."

Harriet turned back to watch the flow of the creek. They sat together in silence a long time.

I have to decide, Harriet thought. Inside her, it felt as if winds were swirling, coming from all angles. She turned Winston's question around and asked herself how it would feel to stay in Boulder. She saw herself passing strangers on the street, even on the path around the lake, seeing them not look up or greet her. She had an image of Joel Peterson's white car parked in front of her condo. I could escape that for a little while she thought, but I mustn't kid myself. She remembered Brenda saying, "Even if you go down there and don't tell anyone what you're doing, doing what you do, people are gonna find you soon enough." She saw her little garden and Tiger on the fence. I'd miss my garden. I'd miss Tiger. But I could get a cat of my own, and there's plenty of room in Mom's backyard to make a new garden. Really, there was little in Boulder to hold her.

She thought more about what it would be like to move to Cottonwood Creek. Living with her mother would be comfortable. They'd always had a close and loving relationship. Her mom would love it if she got a cat. She began to visualize how she would fix up the little yellow house, how the furniture in her Boulder office would fit there. She saw herself hanging out with Sophie and Mary and playing with Mary's little ones. Singing in church again. Being part of a church again, with all that meant in terms of community.

And Winston.

She glanced over at him. He sat quietly beside her, gazing at the creek. Leaf shadows from the tall cottonwood that shaded them played across his face. She felt the deep strength and gentleness of him, remembered his playfulness, and his patient understanding and support through all her turmoil. No matter what other feelings might arise, he was a true friend. Someone she'd like to be with more than just occasionally on a weekend.

Then she remembered that the most important thing was her ulada and the Song. There are other chiropractors in Boulder, she thought, doing good work even if they don't have the Song. Here there is no one. She remembered Neal telling her long ago that he had left the mountains he loved west of Denver to come to Cottonwood Creek because there was need.

With that memory, everything fell into place. She turned to Winston. "I've decided," she said.

He turned to her, question in his eyes.

"I'm coming home. I'll move down here as soon as I can wrap things up in Boulder. Probably in a few months."

He smiled a wide, sweet smile. "I'm glad," he said simply.

As they walked back toward the town, he asked, "Will you sing in church tomorrow?"

"Yes. I'd like to."

Epilogue

It was mid-afternoon on a sunny day in October when Harriet finally arrived in Cottonwood Creek to stay. She pulled into town right behind the moving van, her back seat filled with houseplants and Brenda's two cats hunkered down in their cat crate.

Brenda created quite a stir when she roared into Cottonwood Creek an hour later on her Harley, in her black helmet and black leather jacket, her long gray hair in a single braid down her back. Doors and windows popped open as she zoomed down the quiet streets to the Ellis house.

Harriet's mother welcomed them warmly, and within a few days they were both settled in their new homes. Brenda had bought a house just a few doors from Harriet's new office. It was small, with only one bedroom, but had a shed for the Hog and a garden for the cats, and Brenda was quite pleased with it. Harriet settled in with her mother in the two bedrooms upstairs that had been hers and her sisters' growing up. A few days later, Sophie brought over a small tiger kitten from the latest litter on the ranch.

Harriet's mother was fascinated with the motorcycle. Somewhat to Harriet's trepidation, she accepted Brenda's offer of a ride—and loved it. In the months that followed it was not unusual to see her wearing a shiny blue helmet, riding around town behind Brenda.

Over the preceding summer, Harriet had come down most weekends to be with her mother and supervise the renovation of her little office house. Roger had helped her locate a good painter, and Sophie had driven up to Parker with her to help pick out carpet and curtains. Harriet hired a high school boy who lived two doors down the street to mow and water the lawn and dig up the worst of the weeds.

By the time Harriet arrived in October, the house was painted a soft blue-gray with deep blue trim and a blue door, and the lawn was green and smooth. As soon as she arrived, Harriet planted bulbs in the walkway up to the office and ordered a big wooden sign for the front lawn with Cottonwood Creek Chiropractic painted in the center of a wreath of green leaves.

Inside all was fresh and clean with white walls and blue-green carpet. Harriet had given away almost all the old furniture, so the space was empty and ready for the furniture from her Boulder office, including her electric treatment table. She couldn't bear to get rid of the old treatment table. It came to rest in the upstairs room in her mother's house that she was using for a study, the memories that it evoked woven into the joy and sadness of the Oneness.

During the first week after their arrival, Harriet and Brenda put everything in order in the office. As Harriet went over the patient records of the last five years with Brenda, she found there were still some names she remembered from the days when she had scheduled appointments—long-term patients who had depended on Neal to keep them going all those years.

With much interest, the townspeople watched the preparations for the opening of Cottonwood Creek Chiropractic. They were curious about the tall, quiet woman who was the shoe store owner's daughter, who sang so beautifully in church, and who had now come back to be their doctor.

Winston announced the new practice in church. Brenda called all the patients on Neal's list, and put up notices in the general store, the feed store, and the library. By the time Harriet opened her practice, the first week was already booked.

Harriet decided to make a low-key beginning and kept the Song silent. Still, it did its work, and soon the phone was ringing and people were telling each other all over town that she just laid her hands on them but, afterward, everything was better, even long-term, difficult problems.

Little by little, in certain cases that needed more energy, Harriet began to sing aloud. Word about that soon spread through town. "It's even prettier than when she sings in church," they told each other, "but strange. A strange language."

Harriet was worried that it was only a matter of time before the likes of Joel Peterson found her. She conferred with Brenda. Brenda took over, and asked each patient not to talk about Dr. Ellis's work with anyone from a newspaper or radio, especially not to put anything on the Internet. She told them how Dr. Ellis had been harassed in Boulder and how that had interfered with her work.

Word about that got around, too. The town people felt loyal to their special healer and agreed among themselves they'd all do anything they could to protect her from out-of-town strangers.

Winston came every day to offer support while Harriet and Brenda were setting up the office, and afterward it became a habit for him to stop by at the end of the day to walk Harriet home. As they walked they often talked about the hymn for the following Sunday, which led him to discuss his ideas for the sermon with her. Harriet's mother welcomed him at the door with her usual flutter and often invited him to stay for dinner.

Harriet and Winston never missed their Sunday afternoon walks, or Sunday afternoon tea at the manse as the weather grew colder.

On one mild November afternoon, Harriet took Winston for the first time through the tamarisk and between the tall rocks to her special hideout. They nestled in side by side in the niche overlooking the creek. The sun, though low in the sky, was still warm that day. The cottonwoods were bare, the stream quiet and running low, all nature peaceful as it prepared for the long dormancy of winter.

"This is lovely," Winston said. "I'm honored that you've shared your secret place with me."

"We need a secret place," Harriet said. "People are talking."

"I'm well aware of that. They've been talking about us for a long time. But now that you're here in Cottonwood Creek and I …" He stopped. His cheeks flushed. "Now that you're here and I can't seem to stay away from you for long … well, it's gotten worse."

He shifted his body to face her. "I have a solution. I've been thinking about it for a long time, ever since … Did you know I fell in love with you that very first time we had tea together … and you looked at me with your magical green eyes and asked me if there were angels?" He spoke quickly, his words tumbling out. "We could get engaged. Then it would be totally appropriate for us to spend time together."

A surge of joy and excitement swelled up in Harriet's chest and burst out in her smile. "Engaged?"

"Yes. And then married. Would you?"

Harriet realized that deep inside she had been waiting for that question a long time. "Yes!"

They were wed the following May in a big church celebration that was the beginning of a long, rich, and happy marriage. Harriet moved into the manse and made it a beautiful, welcoming home, not only for her husband, but for all who came there.

Freed from the burden of doubt, Harriet's relationship to the Song evolved. Her understanding, her confidence, and her skill increased. Sometimes, as she worked, she felt that the Song guided her as it had at first, sometimes that she was guiding the Song; gradually it became such a blending that she and the Song moved as one.

Her vision continued to open. Even without touching, even just passing a neighbor on the street, she began to see what the wound was, whether of body or spirit, and how the Song might ease it. She shared her insights with Winston, and they worked together for the healing of their community.

Within the first year of her practice, the Song had touched almost everyone in Cottonwood Creek and the surrounding ranches. Everyone was healthy; no longer was anyone troubled by disease, chronic pain, or even irritating small discomforts. Any injuries or illnesses were quickly mended. Harriet and Winston noticed that as the health of the community increased, so did the peoples' patience, forgiveness, and kindness. Perhaps it was not only the physical healing that changed them, but the love that poured through the Song. Old feuds and petty quarreling faded away. Gossip persisted—how could it not in a small town?—but it became more kindly and helpful.

The people in the town held Harriet in awe. This could have isolated her, but her family and Brenda saw her as they always had, and Winston was always there for her, to share with and confide in.

Together they marveled at the transformation of their community. Harriet began to understand the vision of the Elirians, that without suffering humans could be their best selves, how relieving the suffering could indeed shift the web. She lived in reverence and gratitude that she could be part of that shift.

She thought often of the others in unknown places around the planet who had also received the Song, and wondered how it was for them and the people they touched. At times she could almost sense them, as if the web the Elirians spoke of connected her to them.

Although she knew the Elirians were far away and she could no longer communicate with them telepathically, still she felt their love and presence with her every time the Song moved through her.

Also from Heather Starsong

Never Again

Leaves in Her Hair

The Purest Gold

www.heatherstarsong.com

About the Author

*H*eather Starsong grew up in New England and graduated summa cum laude from Boston University in 1957 with a Bachelor of Arts in Comparative Literature.

She has been a dancer since childhood, especially fascinated with the connections between healing, art, and spirit. She has explored and taught many forms: creative dance, liturgical dance, dance therapy, yoga, ceremonial dance, Rolfing® and Rolf Movement,® Continuum, and most recently Argentine Tango.

Although her career has been focused on body language, she has loved and told stories all her life. In 2007 she began to write her stories. *Leaves in Her Hair* was published in 2009, *Never Again* in 2015, and *The Purest Gold* in 2017.

She is presently semi-retired from a long career of teaching dance and yoga and practicing Rolfing. She lives in Boulder, Colorado, and enjoys writing, dancing, hiking in the high country, and spending time with her grandchildren.

Find out more about Heather Starsong on her web page:
www.heatherstarsong.com